SCOTLAND'S EARLY SILVER

SCOTLAND'S EARLY SILVER
TRANSFORMING ROMAN PAY-OFFS TO PICTISH TREASURES

ALICE BLACKWELL, MARTIN GOLDBERG AND FRASER HUNTER

Scotland's Early Silver

Exhibition at:

National Museum of Scotland
Chambers Street
Edinburgh EH1 1JF

www.nms.ac.uk

13 October 2017 to 25 February 2018

Book published in 2017 by
NMS Enterprises Limited – Publishing
a division of NMS Enterprises Limited
National Museums Scotland
Chambers Street, Edinburgh EH1 1JF

Text and photographic images © National Museums Scotland 2017 (unless otherwise credited: see Acknowledgements page at the end of this book).

Format and additional material
© National Museums Scotland 2017

No part of this publication may be reproduced, stored in a retrieval system or transmitted in any form or by any means, electronic, mechanical, photocopying, recording or otherwise, without the prior written permission of the publisher.

The rights of Alice Blackwell, Martin Goldberg and Fraser Hunter to be identified as the authors of this book have been asserted by them in accordance with the Copyright, Designs and Patents Act 1988.

British Library Cataloguing in Publication Data
A catalogue record for this book
is available from the British Library.

ISBN: 978-1-910682-12-8

Book design and cover by Mark Blackadder.
Printed and bound in Spain by Novoprint, SA, Barcelona.

www.nms.ac.uk
www.glenmorangie.com

THE COVER
The front cover illustration shows Roman hacksilver from Traprain Law, East Lothian.
The rear cover illustration shows Early Medieval hacksilver from Norrie's Law, Fife.

IMAGE CAPTIONS
page II: Roman hacksilver from Traprain Law, East Lothian.
page VII: Early Medieval hacksilver from Norrie's Law, Fife.
page VIII: Roman hacksilver from Traprain Law, East Lothian.
page X: Early Medieval hacksilver from Norrie's Law, Fife.

For a full listing of NMS Enterprises Limited – Publishing titles and related merchandise visit: www.nms.ac.uk/books

Contents

FOREWORD by Dr Gordon Rintoul CBE
NATIONAL MUSEUMS SCOTLAND   IX

FOREWORD by Marc Hoellinger
THE GLENMORANGIE COMPANY   XI

INTRODUCTION   XIII
Silver, not gold

SCOTLAND'S EARLY SILVER

CHAPTER ONE
Sources of silver   3

CHAPTER TWO
Scotland's earliest silver AD 75–160   11

CHAPTER THREE
Bribery beyond *Britannia* AD 140–230   19

CHAPTER FOUR
Silver for changing times AD 250–350   33

CHAPTER FIVE
Pieces of silver:
making sense of the Traprain Treasure AD 350–450   45

CHAPTER SIX

Changing silver for a new world AD 300–500   69

CHAPTER SEVEN

Managing silver, managing change:
Early Medieval hacksilver hoarding AD 400–600   77

CHAPTER EIGHT

New power symbols:
massive silver chains AD 300–500   95

CHAPTER NINE

Holding it together: silver and brooches AD 400–800   107

CHAPTER TEN

New sources and new ideas AD 800–1000   127

CHAPTER ELEVEN

Conclusion: a thousand years of silver   137

BIBLIOGRAPHY   151

EXHIBITED OBJECTS   162

INDEX   164

ACKNOWLEDGEMENTS   171

Foreword

Dr Gordon Rintoul CBE
Director
NATIONAL MUSEUMS SCOTLAND

Today gold is more valuable than silver, but in the first millennium AD silver was the most valued material in Scotland. This new and exotic material arrived with the occupying Roman army and had a lasting impact on Early Medieval society. It changed how people measured and conveyed power and prestige.

Featuring spectacular objects from the first thousand years of silver in Scotland, *Scotland's Early Silver* explores the part this precious metal played in the transformation of society throughout the first millennium AD.

The pioneering partnership between National Museums Scotland and The Glenmorangie Company, founded in 2008, has proven to be an innovative means of supporting research in Early Medieval Scotland and its dissemination. It has been a multi-award winning project of which we are all extremely proud. As with earlier phases of the project, their generous support has also enabled the production of this book and the accompanying exhibition.

I would like to thank our partners at Glenmorangie for their continued support, encouragement and enthusiasm in helping us to cast a new light on this vibrant period of Scotland's past.

EDINBURGH 2017

Foreword

Marc Hoellinger
President and Chief Executive Officer
THE GLENMORANGIE COMPANY

At The Glenmorangie Company we are guided, informed and continually inspired by Scotland's heritage. It is what makes us who we are and it filters through all that we do in crafting our famous whisky. Through the Glenmorangie Research Project, we are extremely proud to have supported National Museums Scotland's ground-breaking work to understand better the people and cultures of Early Medieval Scotland, shedding new light on a critical period of our shared past.

This book takes a fresh approach to Early Medieval Scotland by investigating one important medium – silver. Following this precious and powerful material from its introduction during the Roman period through to the arrival of the Vikings has allowed the Glenmorangie Research Project to reveal more about the people of this period and the world in which they lived. Using National Museums Scotland's outstanding collections, this research has now connected a thousand years of the history of silver in Scotland, exploring fresh evidence and revealing new insights into how this powerful material was used to demonstrate wealth and power and to underpin the new kingdoms of what we now know as Scotland. The Glenmorangie Company is delighted to see the results of this fascinating research presented in this beautiful book.

EDINBURGH 2017

INTRODUCTION
Silver, not gold

Silver was the most precious metal in Scotland for a thousand years. This book tells the story of this powerful material during a pivotal time, from the arrival of the Roman army until the dawn of the Viking Age, 700 years later. We trace silver through changing times, as Roman Iron Age tribal societies gave way to a patchwork of Early Medieval kingdoms. Silver provides a valuable path through this period of transition and social change, a time when historical sources give us few clues and where a firm archaeological footing is rare [Figs 1–6].

Silver first arrived in Scotland with the Roman army in the 1st century AD. Handfuls of silver coins – a soldier's pay packet – and precious dress accessories were the earliest silver objects used in Scotland. From these small beginnings grew a new social order, built on the haves and have-nots, those with and without silver of their own. One hundred years of Roman frontier policy brought substantial quantities of silver coins to the north, gifted to buy off Iron Age tribes beyond their borders [1]. These coins had no monetary value beyond the Roman frontier – instead they had prestige, being used to show off and given as offerings to the gods. Hoarded and buried, this silver was not melted down. But crises in the Roman economy in the 3rd century AD meant that 'silver' coinage contained increasingly little silver, making it an unattractive gift. Instead, hacked-up high-quality silver objects, especially vessels, were turned into bullion [2]; and for the first time in Scotland they began to be recycled into new, local types of objects.

This was the start of generations of recycling – the forging of new status symbols. From elaborate Roman vessels a new Early Medieval language of power was wrought,

Opposite: Roman hacksilver from Dairsie in Fife.

Fig. 1 (above, left): Roman *denarii* from the Falkirk hoard; NMS X.FR 482.

Fig. 2 (above, right): Hacked Roman silver bowl, Dairsie, Fife; NMS X.FRH 2.

Fig. 3 (below, left): Massive silver neck-chain from Borland Farm, Lanarkshire; NMS X.FC 264.

Fig. 4 (below, right): Early Medieval silver brooch with gold wire decoration, Clunie, Perth and Kinross; NMS X.FC 177.

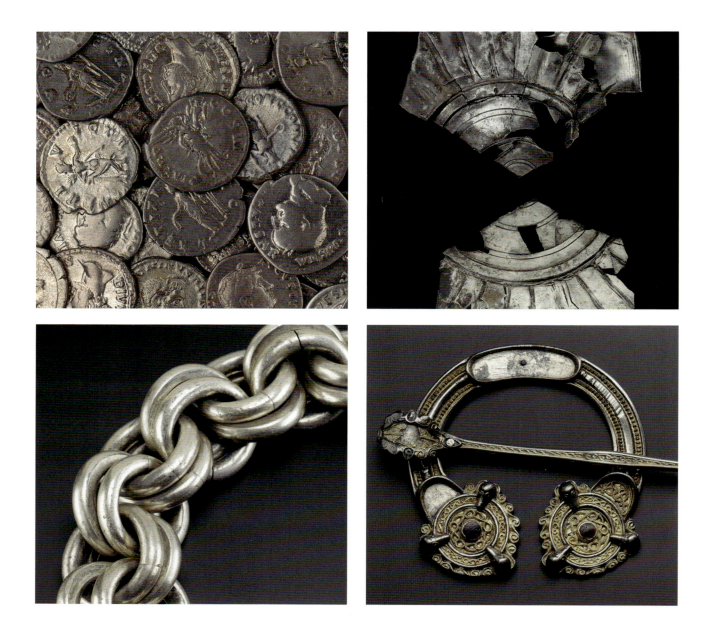

Fig. 5: Fragments of late Roman hacksilver, Traprain Law, East Lothian; NMS X.GVA 44, 142D, 161.

Fig. 6: Late Roman gold and silver coins.

spelled out in massive silver chains [3] and intricately decorated brooches [4]. Worn and buried, hoarded and melted, these objects speak of the transformation of society through the first millennium AD.

Why silver? The answer is a combination of availability and choice. Though the Roman economy relied on gold, Roman foreign policy in Scotland worked almost entirely in silver [5]. This is a sharp contrast with other parts of Europe beyond the Roman frontiers where gold *and* silver were used to buy 'barbarian' allegiance [6]. These different inheritances of Roman metals had implications for what happened next. While in England and on the continent gold became the epitome of Early Medieval wealth and social status [7], in Scotland silver loomed large [8]. Availability always governed its use, but silver was chosen for local expressions of power.

Silver can be valued in different ways. The tipping point between these kinds of value tells of societal and cultural attitudes. When silver was first introduced to Scotland the scales were firmly tipped in favour of social value: this Roman silver was not treated as bullion, not melted down or made into local types of objects. Around the 3rd century AD, the scales tipped the other way, towards bullion value: Roman silver began to be recycled and remade into new types of objects. From then, those using silver had to make a choice – to preserve a silver object, to recycle it, or to take it out of circulation by burying it. Understanding how, when and why these choices were made can tell us a lot about the political and economic history of Iron Age and Early Medieval Scotland. But these ancient choices also have significant implications for interpreting archaeological silver. In the face of failing supplies in a post-Roman world, substantial

INTRODUCTION

Fig. 7: Early Medieval gilded silver brooch from the continent, find-spot unknown; NMS X.FD 35.

Fig. 8: Early Medieval silver brooch from Tummel Bridge, Perth and Kinross; NMS X.FC 162.

ancient recycling has left us with relatively few silver survivals. Very rare hoards give us glimpses of objects that chance saved from the crucible; many are exceptional, even unique.

But this rarity makes understanding objects difficult, restricting our ability to date or provenance key pieces. And the tensions between social and bullion value are not just an issue for deep history. The tipping point between archaeological value and bullion value in the 19th century saw quantities of ancient silver recycled into Georgian and Victorian tableware. Written accounts of the time are the only trace of tantalising treasures lost to the crucible.

This book accompanies a special exhibition, *Scotland's Early Silver*, at the National Museum of Scotland (October 2017–February 2018). The first chapter explores the life-cycle of silver: the sources of raw material, how it was worked into new objects, and how supplies were managed. The chapters thereafter follow the trajectory of silver from its arrival with the Roman army, through its establishment as the Early Medieval power material of choice, to the dawn of the Viking period when new ideas and new sources of silver arrived in Scotland. The final chapter reflects on the role of silver in political and economic developments in Scotland over the course of the first millennium AD. Together they tell a new story of an old metal – one which used to be more powerful than gold.

Fig. 9: Roman hacksilver from Dairsie in Fife.

INTRODUCTION

XVII

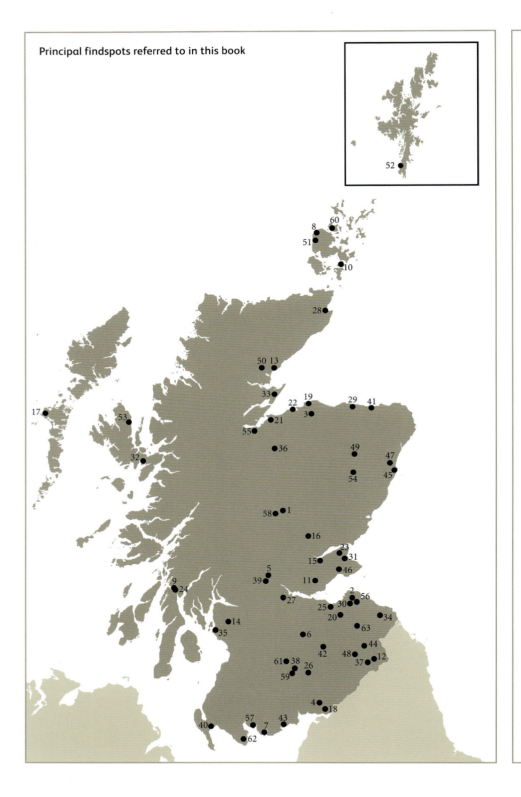

SCOTLAND'S EARLY SILVER

TRANSFORMING ROMAN PAY-OFFS TO PICTISH TREASURES

CHAPTER ONE

Sources of silver

People acquire silver in two ways – by extracting it fresh from the ground, or by recycling old silver objects. In Britain, silver deposits mainly take the form of silver-rich lead ore, known as galena [Fig. 1.1].[1] Getting silver from lead involves significant processing – mining to recover the ore, smelting to retrieve the lead, and refining to separate out the precious metal.[2] The rarity of silver-rich ore and the effort required to extract it from the earth means that recycling has always been an attractive alternative. Turning old silver into new is a much simpler undertaking, involving chopping up objects [1.2] and melting them in ceramic metalworking vessels called crucibles [1.3]. At this stage, recycled silver might be refined (to increase the purity) or debased (by adding base metals in the form of pure copper or recycled copper-alloy objects). The resulting metal can be stored as ingots [1.4] or turned straight into new objects.

Mining for silver in Britain has a long pedigree. Written sources stretch as far back as the Domesday Book, compiled from a survey made in 1086. Several manors in Derbyshire that controlled lead mines were required to pay 40 pounds of pure silver, suggesting the precious metal was being refined from their own lead ore.[3] The exploitation of silver-rich ores in the northern Pennines is attested by written sources from the 1130s,[4] and between 1130 and 1200 an estimated 2,255,000 ounces (around 66 tonnes) of silver was extracted from mines in Cumbria and Northumberland.[5] In 1136, civil war during the reign of the English king Stephen allowed the Scottish king David I (1124–53) to take possession of Carlisle and Cumberland.[6] David I made grants using the revenue from 'his mine of Carlisle' and issued Scotland's first coinage [1.5] – pennies probably

Opposite: Hacked and crushed Early Medieval silver from Norrie's Law, Fife.

Fig.1.1 (above, left): Galena from Wanlockhead, Dumfriesshire; 170mm (height), NMS G.45.85.

Fig. 1.2 (above, right): Hacked silver dish fragment, Traprain Law, East Lothian; 66mm (length), NMS X.GVA 59C.

Fig. 1.3 (below, left): Crucible used for melting silver, Traprain Law, East Lothian; 50mm (height), NMS X.GVM 574.

Fig. 1.4 (below, right): Silver ingot, Gaulcross, Aberdeenshire; 113mm (length).

SCOTLAND'S EARLY SILVER

4

Fig. 1.5: Scotland's first silver coinage – a penny of David I, struck at Carlisle, 1136–53; 20mm (diameter), NMS H.C16455.

minted with Pennine silver. His use of Carlisle silver suggests that Scottish sources were not being exploited during this period. A hundred years later, written sources first document lead mining in Scotland, probably in the Leadhills–Wanlockhead area of South Lanarkshire and Dumfriesshire,[7] but silver extraction is not specifically mentioned until several centuries later still, in 1424.[8] In the 16th and particularly the 17th and 18th centuries, silver deposits were more intensively exploited in the Southern Uplands, the Bathgate Hills (West Lothian), the Ochils (near Alva, Clackmannanshire), and on Islay.[9]

Archaeological and environmental evidence offer other ways of approaching ancient metals use. Lead exploitation can be inferred from the presence of lead ingots, smelting furnaces or slag heaps. Refining silver from lead is achieved by heating metal in small dishes (cupels) to around 1000 degrees centigrade, causing the lead to oxidise and leaving the precious metal behind;[10] both cupel dishes and by-products of the process – lead oxide, known as litharge – can be identified by archaeologists.[11] As well as primary metalworking evidence, lead processing can be inferred from ancient atmospheric pollution. Smelting lead ore causes heavy metal particles to become airborne and then fall to the ground. Samples taken from peat bogs or lake sediments can reveal these metal traces and be dated to fix when the pollution, and therefore the ore processing, occurred.

Intermittent lead use is first found in Scotland in the Bronze Age and Iron Age, but seems to have been a very restricted experiment.[12] Archaeological evidence for lead mining in Roman-period Britain is much more widely attested, from the Mendips, the Derbyshire Peak District, the Welsh/English Marches, north Wales, the Pennines and perhaps south-west Scotland.[13] These sources were clearly valued for silver as well as lead: stamps on Roman lead ingots state that they came from the silver-works, while by-products of the refining process have been recognised at a few Roman sites.[14]

Pollution evidence from several bogs in south-western Scotland suggests lead processing happened nearby during the Iron Age and Roman periods, and again during the 5th–7th centuries and 9th–13th centuries AD, as well as in the later and post-Medieval periods.[15] Lead slag has been found at multiple sites in the Southern Uplands, particularly in the Leadhills–Wanlockhead area, but none of the deposits is dated. Excavations at the 6th–7th century fort of Trusty's Hill in Galloway produced a lead ingot which scientific analysis suggests may have come from an ore source in the Southern Uplands; if correct, this supports

SOURCES OF SILVER

environmental evidence for Early Medieval lead mining in the region.[16] Another Galloway hillfort, the Mote of Mark, produced ceramic vessels used for refining precious metals.[17] Elsewhere in southern Scotland, charcoal associated with lead slag deposits in the Manor Valley, south-west of Peebles in the Scottish Borders, was radiocarbon-dated to the 10th and 11th centuries AD,[18] but whether silver was being refined from this lead is unknown.

Scientific analysis of silver objects provides another clue to ancient metal sources. Lead is unusual because different sources vary in the relative abundance of its four stable isotopes. Scientific analysis can quantify these isotope ratios, producing a fingerprint for specific ore sources that can establish a link between objects and specific mines.[19] Ancient silver retains a small proportion of the lead from which it was extracted, which means lead-isotope analysis can also be used to provenance silver. However, while this method can work for objects made from silver freshly extracted from lead ore, it becomes more difficult once the metal has been recycled. Mixing objects from different ore sources in the same crucible means the isotope signatures become confused and the link to a specific ore source is lost. The limited evidence for lead and silver exploitation during the first millennium AD suggests that Scotland's early silver was recycled rather than freshly mined metal, meaning this technique is of limited use in establishing the geological provenance.

What silver was being recycled in Scotland in the first millennium AD? Substantial payments of Roman silver coins were made to people beyond the Roman frontier in the late 2nd and early 3rd century as part of diplomatic efforts (see chapter 3), but though they were clearly desirable objects there is no evidence that they were melted down. This changed with a shift in Roman policy. With the devaluation of coinage, the Empire switched to making payments in hacked-up Roman plate – beautiful and prestigious tableware that had been cut up for its bullion value.

Two such Roman hacksilver hoards are known from Scotland (see chapters 4 and 5). They survive today because they were buried and not reclaimed, but others must have been lost to the silversmith's crucible, supplying the wealth of later silver. It was Roman hacksilver – like the 23 kilograms of hacked dishes, cups, platters, flagons and spoons from the Traprain Treasure – that was recycled and remade, turned into the first of generations of local prestige objects.

Recycling changed silver. Smiths added small quantities of other metals during the melt, altering the composition of the alloy. Scrap copper alloy was added to make the silver stretch further, or to make a harder and more resilient metal. Today, scientific analysis can examine silver alloys of different dates and provenances (see page 7), and is particularly useful for distinguishing between Roman items (the raw material) and Early Medieval silver objects (the products of recycling). With the collapse of the western Roman Empire, payments to tribes beyond the frontier dried up. No new silver supplies were available in Scotland until the dawn of the Viking Age four hundred years later, meaning that recycling became essential.

Fig. 1.6 (right): A graph comparing tin and gold levels in the silver revealed the presence of undiluted Roman material in the hoard from Norrie's Law. The blue circle shows the composition of the Traprain Law silver, while the red circle shows the more debased Norrie's Law finds. The red triangles represent objects from Norrie's Law with a Roman composition.

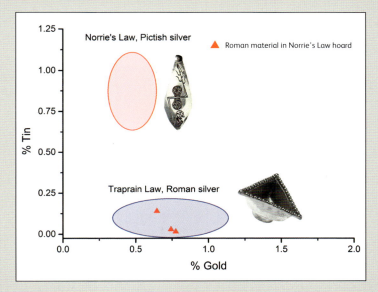

RECYCLING ANCIENT SILVER: A SCIENTIST'S VIEW

Lore Troalen

Scientific analysis of the composition and fineness of silver alloys can reveal their history and how they were made. This is done through technical laboratory examination under a microscope and non-invasive elemental analysis. In some cases we take minute samples to establish how metals were worked.

Two key techniques have been used in our work to establish the composition of the silver. One is X-ray fluorescence (XRF), where high-powered X-rays are fired at an object. This excites the different elements in its surface, resulting in the emission of characteristic secondary X-rays. We can measure both the exact energy emitted (which tells us which elements are present) and the amount (which allows us to quantify the proportions of different components).

Initially we analyse an object with XRF without cleaning the surface, in order to do no damage. However, corrosion of ancient silver alloys affects surface analysis, so the results are not always accurate.[20] One way of getting round this is to take micro-samples of metal, polish them up, and analyse them with a related technique, particle-induced X-ray emission (PIXE). This delivers complementary data to XRF, with much more precise information on minor and trace elements in the alloys which provides clues to provenance and recycling.[21]

We focused on two key hoards, comparing the late Roman hoard from Traprain Law (East Lothian) to the Early Medieval hoard from Norrie's Law in Fife.[22] Late Roman silver is characteristically very pure – around 95% silver, with much of the balance being gold and lead derived from the original ores where it was mined. The composition of the Traprain silver is

	copper	silver	gold	tin	lead	zinc
Traprain Law (mean of 36 objects)	2.5	96.3	0.8	0.03	0.4	0.02
Norrie's Law (mean of 10 objects)	7.3	88.6	0.5	0.9	0.8	1.3

Fig. 1.7 (above): Mean composition (percentage by weight) of Traprain Law and Norrie's Law silver, determined by PIXE analysis on clean micro-samples (data from Tate and Troalen 2009).

very similar to other late Roman silver.[23] Early Medieval silver has seen much less research, but we were able to show that the Norrie's Law material was more debased, with noticeable traces of copper, tin, lead and zinc [1.6, 1.7].[24] It appears that the original Roman silver was diluted by adding some copper alloy in order to extend the amount of silver available, reducing its purity as a result.

But we found a twist to this story. Some of our results from Norrie's Law were quite unexpected – there was more material matching the composition of Roman silver amongst the hoard's contents than had been realised. Several small fragments were undiagnostic to the eye, but their composition showed they were clearly made from undiluted Roman silver. This scientific analysis has taken us beyond the naked eye, giving insights into the legacy of Roman silver.

Opposite: Hacked Roman silver from Traprain Law.

NOTES

1. The lead minerals most commonly exploited in antiquity were galena (lead sulphide) and cerussite (lead carbonate). 'Native' silver – silver particles adhering to another mineral – is rare, though significant amounts were mined from Alva (Clackmannanshire) in the 18th century. Virtually no silver is produced in the United Kingdom today, bar small quantities from Northern Ireland (Idoine et al. 2016, 73).
2. Lead carbonate also requires roasting before smelting.
3. Allen 2011, 115.
4. The English Crown controlled the collection of mines in Tynedale known as the 'mine of Carlisle' where silver mining is attested from the 1130s; the bishop of Durham controlled silver exploitation in north-west England. Today, rights to mine silver and gold in most of the United Kingdom are held by the Crown, with a few exceptions that include the former County of Sutherland, retained by the Duchy of Sutherland.
5. Claughton 2003. Recently, these estimates have been reconsidered and Allen (2011) has argued that in fact imported silver (rather than that from the northern Pennines) was usually a greater source of the metal in English currency during 1086–1500.
6. Barrow 1973, 142–8.
7. Harvey 1997, 124. He also noted a reference to the movement of lead from there to Rutherglen in 1264.
8. Harvey 1997, 126; Cochran-Patrick 1876, 45. The first record of the discovery of gold in Scotland dates to 1245, reported by Gilbert de Moravia from Durness (Sutherland): Clark 2014, 1.
9. Wilson and Flett 1921.
10. The process can be further complicated if silica is present – high quantities can stop the smelting process unless higher temperatures and more strongly reducing conditions are achieved (Kassiandou 2003, 198).
11. Litharge can indicate refining of recycled silver as well as extraction from galena.
12. A string of lead beads on an Early Bronze Age necklace from West Water Reservoir in Peeblesshire represents the earliest lead known in Britain and Ireland; analysis indicated a Southern Uplands source. It most likely stems from an experimental phase of early metallurgy; lead saw very little use for artefacts until the Roman period, although some must have been in circulation as it was used regularly in the Late Bronze Age as an alloying element in bronze castings (it is markedly rarer in the Iron Age). Another experimental episode is represented by some extraordinary lead beads from an Iron Age fort at Carghidown in Wigtownshire; the site sits close to a known non-ferrous metal source (Hunter and Davis 1994, 2000; Hunter 2007c).
13. Tylecote 1986, 61–70; Collingwood and Wright 1991a, 38–66; Mattingly 2006, 506–8; Newman 2016, 20. The distribution of stamped lead ingots and industrial debris in relation to known ore sources provide the main clues to industrial centres. No such evidence is yet known from Scotland, but isotopic analysis of an unstamped lead ingot from Strageath (Perthshire) suggested it came from the Wanlockhead area in the Southern Uplands (Gardiner 2001, 13; Hunter 2006, 85).
14. Including Pentrehyling fort (Shropshire), Wroxeter and Chichester; Bayley and Eckstein 1998; Bayley, Dungworth and Paynter 2001, 3; Bayley 2009.
15. Mighall et al. 2014; Kuttner et al. 2014.
16. Pashley and Evans 2017.
17. Probable cupels were found, though they could be unusually large crucibles (Laing and Longley 2006, 25–6). Parting vessels, used to separate gold from silver, were also recovered. Parting involved heating the silver–gold alloy and adding salt which attacked the silver, forming silver chloride which was absorbed by the walls of the ceramic parting vessel, leaving the pure gold behind. The silver could then be extracted from the clay (Tylecote 1986, 60–1).
18. Pickin 2010. Interestingly these sites were around 8 km from the nearest lead sources. Tenth-century lead smelting sites have also been identified recently in Cumbria: Fairburn 2007; Smith 2006.

19. Unlike most chemical elements, the stable isotopes of lead are still being formed today through the decay of radioactive substances. In lead, two isotopes are derived from uranium, and one from thorium; the fourth is no longer being radioactively generated. This radiogenesis happens continuously until the lead ore is deposited, meaning that every ore source will have a unique ratio of the four stable isotopes. At present, the main method used to analyse these isotopic ratios is MC-ICP-MS or multicollector inductively coupled plasma mass spectrometry. In the last forty years there has been debate about application of stable lead-isotope analysis in establishing metal provenance. Recent studies have established its use and addressed the issues highlighted by earlier practitioners. See Stos-Gale and Gale (2009) for a review of recent debates on the methodology and application of lead isotope analysis, and Ellis (2000, 311–19) for an overview of the method. Recent refinements in the method are presented in Baron, Tamas and Le Carlier (2014).
20. Tate 1986; Beck et al. 2004; Tissot et al. 2016.
21. The PIXE work was undertaken at the AGLAE accelerator facility, based in the C2RMF laboratory in Paris. This work was made possible thanks to a grant from the European FP5 EU-Artech project.
22. Tate and Troalen 2009.
23. Lang, Hughes and Oddy 1984; Hughes et al. 1989; Bennett 1994; Hook and Callewaert 2013; Doračić, Lang and Fletcher 2015; Lang and Hughes 2016.
24. Tate and Troalen 2009.

CHAPTER TWO

Scotland's earliest silver

AD 75–160

The handful of silver coins plucked from a Borders field glint and gleam as you turn them to the light. They bear faces, mostly male, on the front and varied designs on the back – ships, military standards, and a bewildering range of gods and goddesses. Some were struck by the mint in Rome long before the armies came to Scotland in the late 70s AD, their surfaces smoothed from countless long-forgotten transactions as goods and services were bought and sold. To the Roman army of occupation, these were daily currency. But to the locals in this freshly-occupied land we call Scotland, this was an exotic, unexpected new material. With the Roman armies, silver reached Scotland.[1]

'Roman Scotland' is a misnomer. Scotland was never a full part of the Roman world. The south of Scotland was occupied on at least three occasions, part of the martial edge of the Roman Empire. There were no towns or villas here. Instead there was a network of forts, most garrisoned by 500 or 1000 heavily-armed soldiers. In these forts and the settlements which clustered around them to provide for their needs, silver was a regular feature, mostly as coinage, more rarely for other items such as jewellery. But in the surrounding farms where locals continued their lives in parallel to this Roman intrusion, and in the lands to the north where 'barbarians' lurked, silver was exceptional. We need to consider silver in these two different worlds.

The Roman world, from the Empire's heart to the forts on the frontier's edge, ran on a market economy lubricated by coinage [Fig. 2.1]. Loose change in your pocket was a series of different bronze coins, used to buy food or gamble on a dice game. Gold coins were a rarity, kept for hoarding wealth; a frontier soldier would rarely see one. For them, wealth was silver. Troops were primarily paid in silver –

Opposite: Silver coins (*denarii*) from the Roman fort of Newstead in the Scottish Borders.

Fig. 2.1: The coins from a Roman pocket – different denominations of silver and bronze coins from the Roman fort of Newstead in the Scottish Borders. A gold coin (*aureus*) was worth 25 silver coins (*denarii*), or 100 of the largest bronze coins (*sestertii*).

Fig. 2.2: Romano-British silver trumpet brooch from Ayrshire. Its precise findspot is unknown, so it is unclear if it comes from a Roman site or had reached local hands; 74mm (length), NMS X.FG 9.

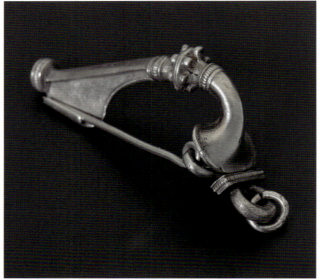

250 *denarii* (silver coins) per year in the 70s AD for the typical frontier infantry soldier, rising to 500 around AD 197 as inflation (and the need to ensure the army's loyalty) took its toll.[2] So a single *denarius* was around a day's pay. You might drop a bronze coin and barely pause for thought, but you'd stop and search for a missing silver one.[3]

Silver was handled regularly as coinage, but was otherwise rare. It was a prestigious metal in the Roman world. Ordinary brooches were copper alloy – special ones were silver [2.2].[4] So too with tableware, where silver vessels were the preserve of the élite, while silver finger-rings were rare compared to iron or bronze ones. On a Roman site, silver objects marked out people of status [2.3, 2.9].[5]

This sense of the importance of silver was transferred to the local population. They met this new metal in their dealings with Rome, not all of which took place at the point of a sword. The Roman army needed to do more than

SCOTLAND'S EARLY SILVER

Fig. 2.3: Part of a silver necklace from Newstead Roman fort in the Scottish Borders. The crescent and wheel pendants probably represent the sun and moon; 26mm (wheel diameter), NMS X.FRA 851.

fight. Emissaries built diplomatic relations to help keep the peace, negotiated for supplies – and taxed the inhabitants of this freshly-conquered territory. The locals had no tradition of coin use: they occasionally encountered these strange shiny discs, but they appeared of little value to a people who did not spend money.[6] More interesting were things they could actually use, such as Roman silver jewellery which could be worn to impress. The gem-set finger-ring from Culbin Sands in Moray [2.4] was found far beyond the Roman frontier and would have marked out the owner as a person of substance with wide-ranging connections.[7] But such finds are rare – three further rings from Capledrae (Fife [see 4.3]), Luce Sands (Wigtownshire), and Traprain Law (East Lothian), two ear-rings from Traprain, animal-headed bracelets from Macduff (Aberdeenshire [2.5]) and Hallow Hill (Fife), and brooches from Athelstaneford (East Lothian), Carn Liath (Sutherland) and Tarland (Aberdeenshire) are the sum total of silver jewellery beyond the Roman world; while a curious miniature strainer from the hillfort of Traprain Law is a Roman religious item, perhaps brought to the site as a good luck charm [2.6].[8]

So silver, this new shiny metal, met an interested audience. In the status-conscious world of the Iron Age it came to take on a key role.

SCOTLAND'S EARLIEST SILVER

Fig. 2.4 (above, left): Roman silver finger-ring from Culbin Sands, Moray, with a gem showing the god Silvanus; 10mm (gem height), NMS X.BI 29463.

Fig. 2.5 (below): Roman gilt silver ram-headed terminal, perhaps from a bracelet, found near Macduff, Aberdeenshire; 24mm (length). University of Aberdeen Museums. Image © National Museums Scotland.

Fig. 2.6 (above, right): Miniature Roman silver strainer, probably a votive model, from Traprain Law, East Lothian; 33mm (length), NMS X.GVM 261.

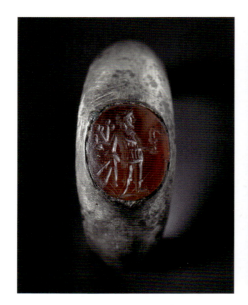

SCOTLAND'S EARLY SILVER

Fig. 2.7 (right): The unusual silver coin hoard from Elginhaugh in Midlothian; NMS X.1998.1–45.

Fig. 2.8 (below): Names of different legions on coins of Mark Antony from the Elginhaugh hoard.

MORE THAN MONEY: AN UNUSUAL HOARD FROM A ROMAN FORT

In the late 1980s, archaeologists were hard at work on a building site at Elginhaugh, near Dalkeith to the south of Edinburgh. The site was scheduled for development – its last known occupants had been the Roman army, 1900 years previously. A fort for 500 cavalry soldiers had been built there in the late AD 70s and occupied for about a decade.[9]

The site produced a lot of new information – it is the most completely excavated fort anywhere in the Roman Empire. One of the most intriguing finds was a small hoard of 45 *denarii* found in the foundations of the headquarters building [2.7]. This was no ordinary stash of silver, drawn randomly from circulating coinage – it was a very particular selection. While ten were recently minted, the remainder were antiques, over one hundred years old when they were buried – the oldest had been struck in 115 BC. Not only that, but almost every antique coin was different.[10] It looks like a deliberate collection where someone has tried hard to get a range of different 'heads'. This was a coin-collector's hoard.[11]

We can see this clearly in one particular coin type – *denarii* of Mark Antony, the lover of Cleopatra, who struck a series of coins to pay his army in 32–31 BC in the run-up to his final battle with the future emperor Augustus [2.8]. They featured a ship on one side and legionary standards on the other, with specific legions named. If you take a random handful of these coins, you're likely to get some duplicates – just like modern Panini football stickers. Yet here, it seems every legion is different (some are a little worn, so we can't be entirely sure). Someone was collecting a set of legions.

Why was it buried? It was found in the foundations of the headquarters, the logistical and symbolic heart of the site where

pay was safeguarded and the unit's standards were kept. This unusual hoard was not simply hidden in an inaccessible foundation trench – it was a deliberate offering to the gods when the building was erected, intended to bring luck to this exposed frontier fort on the Empire's edge.[12] Silver coins could represent much more than just money.

SCOTLAND'S EARLIEST SILVER

NOTES

1. Southern England saw silver jewellery and coinage in the late Iron Age, most likely from recycled Roman Republican coinage (e.g. Dennis 2008; Cottam et al. 2010), but this had little impact in the north of Britain. A single Gaulish coin of the 1st century BC from a garden in Clarkston (Glasgow) may well be a modern rather than an ancient loss (Hunter 1997, 514). Recent excavations at Knowe of Skea on Westray found crucibles with traces of silver-working which may represent a precocious phase of silver recycling, but its precise dating and significance are still under study (G Wilson, pers. comm.)
2. Auxiliary cavalrymen and legionary infantry were better paid, increasing from 300 to 600 *denarii* over the same period. Officers were paid substantially better than troops (Campbell 1994, 20; Speidel 1992, table 7; cf. Alston 1994, arguing legionary and auxiliary pay was the same). Creighton's (2014) subtle analysis of *denarius* hoards from Britain confirms the flow of silver to the army, with newly-minted coinage preponderant in military areas. The wooden writing tablets from Vindolanda provide insights into the workings of the frontier economy: see Grønlund Evers 2011, esp. 20–4.
3. Reece 1984, 201–2. See also Richard Reece's useful discussion of ancient evidence for the value of coinage; Reece 2002, 107–26.
4. Only 6 of the 500 Roman brooches known from Scotland are silver. The exact findspot of the silver trumpet brooch in Fig. 2.2 is not known; the account of its purchase records, 'It is stated to have been found in Ayrshire, the precise locality being unknown' (*Proceedings of the Society of Antiquaries of Scotland* 19 (1884–5), 332; Black 1895, 9–10, fig. 5).
5. There are passing references to certain materials for rings being restricted to particular social classes – gold was for senators, for instance, in the early Empire (Henig 2007, 12). Silver is not mentioned specifically, but the low percentage of silver rings confirms it was restricted. A survey of over 3000 rings from France found copper alloy predominated (62.3%), with 16% gold, 10.3% silver, 6.5% iron and 4.9% other materials (Guiraud 1989, fig. 54); of 700 1st–2nd century rings in southern Britain, 9% were gold, 10% silver, 21% iron, 60% copper alloy (Cool 2000, 32). It is likely that iron was originally markedly more common, but its preservation is poor. This is well illustrated by finds recorded by the Portable Antiquities Scheme, overwhelmingly from metal-detecting: on 15 June 2017, their database [www.finds.org.uk] included 114 gold rings, 534 silver, 2064 copper alloy – and 4 of iron.
6. Over 230 Scottish Iron Age sites have produced Roman finds, but only around 40 have produced coins of the 1st–2nd century, mostly in very small numbers. They show a preference for higher-value gold and silver. The ratio of gold:silver:copper alloy is 2:22:23 coins (in percentages 4%:47%:49%). For comparison, the same ratio for the large Roman assemblage from Newstead is 1.5%:43.5%:55% (from Holmes 2012, table 1; 360 coins).
7. Henig 2007, 103, no. 99.
8. Capledrae [Fig. 4.3] is a recent unpublished find (Fife Cultural Trust Collections). Luce Sands: Wilson 2001, 116, fig. 6 W25/6. Traprain Law: Burley 1956, nos 149–50 (ear-rings), 157 (finger-ring), 261 (strainer). Macduff: *Discovery & Excavation in Scotland* 2015, 20. Hallow Hill: Proudfoot 1996, 418. Athelstaneford: Hunter 2009a, 262, fig. A2.2D. Carn Liath (see page 35). Waulkmill: Bradley et al. 2016, 43–4, fig. 3.22.
9. Hanson 2007a for the full report, reviewed by Hodgson 2009; Hanson 2007b for a summary.
10. There are two coins of Julius Caesar, and two possible duplicates among the legionary *denarii* of Mark Antony, though this is not certain. Otherwise all Republican coins were struck by different moneyers and all legionary *denarii* are of different legions.
11. See Bateson and Hanson 1990; Bateson 2007, 263–70.
12. The interpretation has been questioned: Woolliscroft (2017) raised questions about the details of the deposit. Nevertheless, his alternatives for its deposition lack corroborating evidence, and the combination of unusual coins in a symbolic place suggests it was most plausibly an offering.

Fig. 2.9: A selection of Roman silver objects, from Ayrshire, Cappuck, Culbin Sands, Newstead and Traprain Law.

CHAPTER THREE
Bribery beyond *Britannia*
AD 140–230

The tractor trained its floodlight onto the well-wrapped archaeologists as they scraped away the last dregs of plough-soil in the evening's chill. It was barely two hours since the metal-detector had led us to this spot. Initially, Roman coins turned up as singletons, well-spaced, but as the topsoil was carefully sliced away more and more *denarii* appeared, forming a rough line where the plough had dragged them – and then, from one spot, three coins along with pieces of hand-made pottery. The hoard had come back up for air.

Working well past natural light, we removed loose coins and cleaned up the plough-damaged pot with its precious cache of *denarii*. Photographs of the find were taken for the record, a few sips of malt were taken for warmth, and then the hoard was lifted intact in a soil block, for forensic disentangling back in the Museum's conservation labs [Fig. 3.1].

And we started to ponder. Why was it here? In a field at Birnie, near Elgin on the Moray Firth coast, 300 kilometres north of the Roman frontier? On an Iron Age settlement, a society with no currency economy and with little previous interest in Roman coins, as we have seen? What was going on?

The key factor is time. Study of the coins showed that the latest ones were struck in the AD 190s, thirty years after the main Roman occupations of Scotland had ended. The army had abandoned the Antonine Wall across the Forth–Clyde isthmus and pulled back to Hadrian's Wall, with some outpost forts to the north. The whole country north of the Cheviots now lay beyond the Roman world. Sparse historical sources hint at unrest – unusual for a Roman propaganda machine set to produce relentless good news.

Opposite: The hoard of *denarii* found at Falkirk; NMS X.FR 482.

Fig 3.1: Conservation in progress on the first hoard of coins from Birnie.

Fig. 3.2: Distribution of Roman *denarius* hoards north of Hadrian's Wall, excluding those linked to Roman sites.

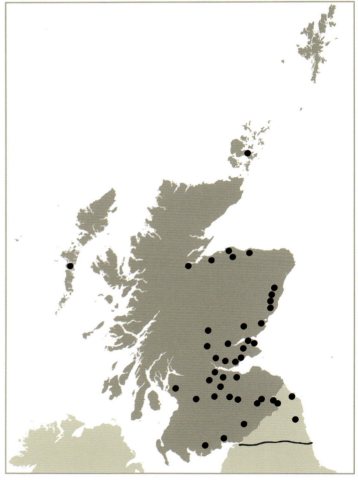

The Roman historian Dio Cassius recorded that under the Emperor Commodus, in AD 182–4:

> *The greatest war ... was in Britain. For the tribes in the island crossed the wall that separated them from the Roman army and did a great amount of damage, even cutting down a general along with his troops*.[1]

The Roman frontier was in trouble.

One solution was military – send in the troops to beat some sense into these restless natives. This was tried,[2] but the army was stretched thin due to problems in other areas closer to the Empire's heartlands. Occasional punitive expeditions would normally quell an area for a generation or more,[3] but Caledonia was in uproar and the available troops were not enough.

There was another time-served tactic – bribery. Diplomatic approaches used sweeteners or subsidies to persuade friendly groups to act as a buffer, or 'gifts' to win round foes. The terminology is deliberately inexact: one side's payment

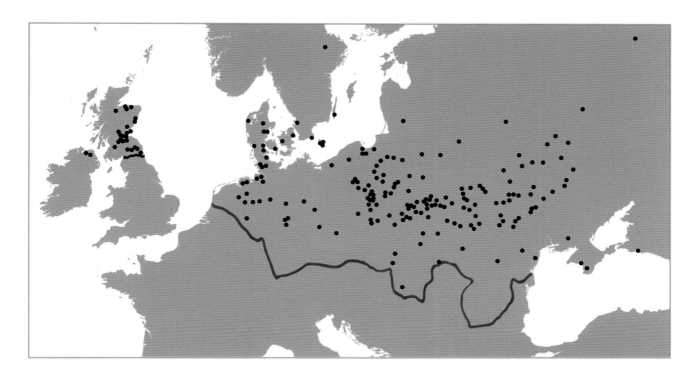

Fig. 3.3: *Denarius* hoards beyond the Roman frontier in Europe. From Lind (1981) with additions for Britain and Ireland. See note 6. Only hoards with over 20 coins are plotted.

is another's pay-off. But the idea was effective. For centuries, the Roman world had built alliances beyond its frontier, sometimes as a precursor to take-over, sometimes as a practical solution when troops were needed elsewhere. Their main tool was silver coinage.[4]

In less than a hundred years, from AD 140–230, we know of 41 hoards of silver coins buried in Scotland, totalling over 6000 coins [3.2]; further examples are reported regularly by responsible metal-detectorists.[5] This is, of course, only the surviving tip of a large silver iceberg, but the quantities show that sending silver north was a widespread policy. Findspots indicate they had come into the hands of local groups. They turn up on Iron Age settlement sites (as at Birnie), in sacred sites such as bogs, and in hidden places whose significance is now irrevocably lost.

For a society that had shown little interest in coinage before, local Iron Age groups were doing a pretty rapid reversal in their views.

In large measure this was driven by Roman policy. The Empire used pay-offs of silver coinage all along its northern frontier as a diplomatic tool at this time [3.3] – hoards of this period are found from Ireland to Russia.[6] For Scotland, we even have a specific reference to the policy. In AD 197 we get a rare snapshot of practical frontier diplomacy in relation to two central Scottish tribes, the Caledonians and the Maeatae:

Since the Caledonians did not remain true to their promises and had made preparations to assist the Maeatae, and since at the time Severus [the Emperor] *was embroiled in war elsewhere, Lupus* [the Governor of Britain] *was forced to buy peace from the Maeatae for a large sum, and in exchange recovered a few captives.*[7]

Fig. 3.4: *Denarius* of Septimius Severus from one of the Birnie hoards.

Some northern European societies already valued silver; others came to value it. But why? What use was money which couldn't be spent? The answer is two-fold: it was an exotic material which could not be obtained in any other way; and it marked the holder as a person with the favour of the Roman world. This was not money to spend, but silver to show off with. It was a marker of status, prestige and connections, used to brandish at ceremonies and at meetings, perhaps to give in gifts to dependants, to seal alliances, or to bribe warriors. It could also be offered as sacrifices to the gods – a likely explanation for the burial of this valuable material.[8] Silver coins didn't circulate as singletons in north-east Scotland – individual coins are almost never found. They moved in bulk.[9] Quantity was everything.

There are unusual features to silver use in Scotland at the time. Such coins might seem a handy raw material to be melted down and converted into local prestige goods. Yet curiously there is no evidence of this – despite searching excavation archives and analysing moulds and crucibles for traces of silver, there was very little locally-made silver at this period.[10] Perhaps it was the very essence of these coins which mattered more – an exotic material bearing the face of the emperor himself [3.4].[11] Local Iron Age societies had no such art – there was no tradition of naturalistic depictions of humans or gods. Indeed, it seems to have been taboo in local traditions to show recognisable people. Instead, Celtic art was full of shape-shifting hints of creatures, not portraits of real men.[12] In both material and image, these coins had a power which ensured they were preserved whole. They may even have been seen as sacred. Recycling, it seems, is a later part of our story.

Throughout northern Europe this Roman silver had a prestige value. It turns up on local power centres, and local copies were made to augment the supplies. These circulated from the Black Sea to Scandinavia, showing the extent of networks beyond the Roman frontier at the time.[13] Such copies didn't reach Scotland, but we may have our own variants, for ceramic moulds to make imitation Roman coins have been found on a few sites [3.5]. However, these were more likely involved in fraudulent transactions with the Roman world, for most of the findspots are in southern Scotland, well connected with the frontier by road or sea.[14] These moulds also lie south of the core area of *denarius* hoards, so were not supplying a local demand.

This is a key point – silver coins were not sent to the whole of Scotland. They were carefully targeted to selected groups in southern and eastern Scotland up to the Moray

Fig. 3.5: Ceramic moulds for making fake Roman *denarii* from Brighouse Bay, Dumfries and Galloway, and Newstead in the Scottish Borders; 25 mm (diameter of left mould), NMS X.1997.770 and X.2017.64.

Firth [3.2]. This pattern is quite different from earlier times: in the later 1st and earlier 2nd centuries, Roman finds occurred across the whole of Scotland. But this more focused distribution fits the politics of the later 2nd century. Roman literary sources indicate recurring problems on the northern frontier, culminating in campaigns against the Caledonians and the Maeatae, who lived in Stirlingshire and Perthshire. We still see traces of them in today's placenames: Dunkeld means Fort of the Caledonians, Schiehallion is the Fairy Hill of the Caledonians, while Dumyat Hill near Stirling is derived from the Fort of the Maeatae.[15] The coin hoards occur in the trouble-spots themselves and to the immediate north and south, perhaps to create friendly buffers as well as sweetening the malcontents.[16]

We can see subtle changes in the policy over time, suggesting a good knowledge of the political situation on the ground. One of the great benefits of coin hoards is that they can be dated quite accurately from the overall make-up of the hoard as well as the date of the latest coin.[17]

If we plot these on maps by their date, we find their distribution varies [3.6a–d]. When the Antonine Wall was still occupied very few silver bribes were used [3.6a], but this changed once the Wall was abandoned. Initial diplomatic efforts focused around the trouble-makers in Stirling and Perth [3.6b], but then shifted to their neighbours in Fife, Aberdeenshire and Moray, perhaps in an attempt to create a buffer around the trouble-spots [3.6c]; it seems direct pay-offs were not working. By the early 3rd century the focus had shifted south, to central and southern Scotland [3.6d]: dealings with the more northern tribes had been given up (or been rejected), and the Roman focus was now on Hadrian's Wall and the lands immediately to its north.[18]

There was another factor at play at this time – the army. As we have seen, north Britain had been a nuisance for some years, and in the early 3rd century AD matters came to a head. The emperor himself decided to head for the frontier, with a massive army of some 40,000 troops.[19] Septimius Severus [3.4] set up base in York and fought two campaigns against the troublesome Caledonians and Maeatae, but even the biased Roman sources suggest these were far from successful.[20] Yet the Roman propaganda machine produced

BRIBERY BEYOND *BRITANNIA*

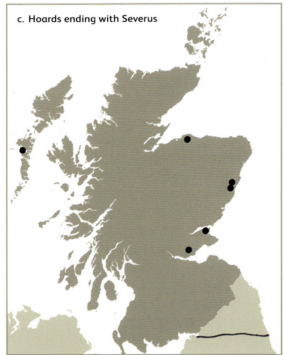

3.6 a. Hoards ending with Antoninus Pius
b. Hoards ending with M Aurelius or Commodus
c. Hoards ending with Severus
d. Hoards ending AD 211–38

Figs 3.6 a–d (opposite): The changing distribution of *denarius* hoards over time.

Fig. 3.7 (below, left): Propaganda coins struck after the Emperor Severus and his son Caracalla campaigned in Scotland, celebrating their supposed victory. The coins show the goddess Victory, trophies of captured weaponry, and barbarian prisoners; NMS C.11742, C.11750, X.1995.84 and X.1996.265–6.

Fig. 3.8 (right): Scotland's largest *denarius* hoard, of almost 2000 coins, which was buried in a Roman pot near the Antonine Wall at Falkirk. The latest coin dates to AD 230, long after the Wall was abandoned. These coins had been given to a local leader; NMS X.FR 482.

coins and sculptures celebrating the 'great victories' [3.7]. Severus died in York in AD 211, and his elder son Caracalla rapidly 'came to terms with the barbarians'[21] – a phrase of compromise quite at odds with the triumphalism of Roman propaganda images. These 'terms' probably involved the movement of silver. Certainly payments continued to groups in southern Scotland for twenty years after this invasion [3.8].

But what effect did these coins have? They may well have proved catastrophic for the local societies involved. Getting Roman silver was not just a lucky lottery win – you became drawn into the Roman web. Not all areas were favoured; Roman policy deliberately sought to create haves and have-nots in order to generate strife and conflict among local groups, who would be less likely to attack the Romans if they were fighting among themselves. Roman sources provide multiple instances of pro-Roman leaders falling to anti-Roman factions.[22] The policy was even more invidious. The Roman world gave large amounts of silver to people in north-east Scotland, and then cut off the supply. People and groups who had grown quite dependent on Roman silver as a way of showing off suddenly discovered how manipulative this Empire could be. This silver had become a key power-tool for local society; suddenly it was scarce. It seems there was not a deep enough local reservoir of silver to keep this prestige economy going. In other parts of northern Europe, *denarii* were saved for centuries in family treasuries. Some Danish *denarii* were so heavily used they are worn almost smooth, and were finally buried up

BRIBERY BEYOND *BRITANNIA*

Fig. 3.9 (opposite): Aerial photograph of the Birnie Iron Age settlement. In the ripening barley, dark circles can be seen where Iron Age houses once stood. The crop ripens more slowly where the soil is deeper, for instance where a pit or posthole was dug into subsoil. © Moray Aerial Survey (Barri Jones / Ian Keillar).

to 400 years after they reached Scandinavia.[23] In Belgium, the rich grave of the Merovingian king Childeric, who died around AD 475,[24] contained a treasure of over 200 *denarii* which were three hundred years old by this point.[25] But in Scotland there is no trace of these Roman coins remaining in circulation. This was a boom and bust economy: the new wealth came in and was exchanged, flaunted and buried, for safety or as religious offerings, giving thanks for good times or seeking help in bad ones. But the time of plenty was short.

The effects of this interplay with Rome seem to have been disastrous. All across north-east Scotland we see major changes in the decades around AD 200. Long-lived settlements which had been occupied for generations fell into decay. Time-honoured architectural traditions were abandoned. For almost two thousand years, the resilient roundhouse, of timber, turf and sometimes stone, had been the standard house type. But no new roundhouses were built. Typical, distinctive local styles of jewellery in metal or glass ceased to be made. Archaeologically we hit a blank period – a virtual dark age. For two or three hundred years, we struggle to find settlements, houses or artefacts. And as hints of evidence re-emerge, they are different. People were living in different places, in different styles of houses which left few archaeological traces. Some of the jewellery shows links to older forms, but it had changed. The big, bold ornaments so typical of the 1st and 2nd centuries AD were replaced by small, subtle brooches and pins.[26]

Archaeologists still argue over what exactly happened, and why. Traditionally it has been suggested that small-scale tribes came together in the face of the Roman threat to form larger political groups which came to be called the Picts, posing a major military problem for the Romans through the 4th century.[27] But there are problems with this amalgamation argument, especially the evidence for widespread abandonment of settlements and of architectural traditions which point to major social dislocation. More likely, Roman interference destabilised local societies beyond a tipping point. Some people got rich, others did not, creating resentment; then even the rich started to struggle as Roman favour moved on. From this, an anti-Roman faction came to power, determined to cause trouble in the Roman world. If we look to recent history, indigenous peoples often fare badly when they meet empires. We don't just need to think of Native Americans, Maori or Aboriginals, who lost land and culture to an occupying power; consider the Inuit, beyond the edge of most colonial interests, and yet still gravely affected by their interactions with the western world. Empires have a big impact far beyond their formal borders, whether intentional or not, shaking up many aspects of neighbouring societies.[28]

In the short term, the Roman policy worked, from their point of view. The historical sources suggest the British frontier was peaceful for the rest of the 3rd century, in contrast to the German frontier which was in turmoil at the time.[29] But the relief was to be short-lived.

BIRNIE: LOCAL POWER AND ROMAN SILVER

An unremarkable field at Birnie, near Elgin in Moray, produced a rich harvest of silver coins – and excavations have allowed archaeologists to reveal the history of this remarkable find.

The first *denarii* were found by metal-detectorist Hamish Stuart in the mid-1990s [3.10]. They were reported through the Treasure Trove system and attracted the attention of the National Museum. This field was known to contain an Iron Age settlement: an aerial photograph taken by the Moray Aerial Survey had revealed marks in the growing barley that showed a pattern of roundhouses, typical of the Iron Age [3.9]. But there was nothing to distinguish it from dozens of similar sites

– until the coins appeared. Excavations by National Museums Scotland from 1998–2011[30] exposed a large area of the site with a long history – a slice through time showing how this part of the Moray coastal plain was used over thousands of years, and revealing an Iron Age settlement of rare importance.

The field saw activity of some sort in the Neolithic period (*c.* 4000–3000 BC) and early Bronze Age (*c.* 2500–2000 BC), and was the site of a short-lived bronze-casting workshop in the late Bronze Age (*c.* 1000–800 BC). But the focus of activity was

Fig. 3.10 (right): Two of the first *denarii* found at Birnie which indicated the presence of a coin hoard. The fresh coin on the left is of the Emperor Commodus; the worn one on the right of Vespasian was over a hundred years old when it was buried.

BRIBERY BEYOND *BRITANNIA*

27

Fig. 3.11: Excavating a burnt-down round-house at Birnie.

Fig. 3.12: The first *denarius* hoard found at Birnie. It had been damaged by the plough, and included at least 320 coins, the latest of AD 196.

during the later Iron Age, *c.* 200 BC–AD 200, when a major village developed. The houses were massive, complicated constructions of timber and turf up to 20 metres in diameter, each probably home to an extended kin-group of 15–20 people and their animals [3.11]. Additional buildings served as stores and workshops; there was evidence of a wide range of crafts at the site, from everyday tasks such as potting, textile and leather production, to much rarer skills such as the smelting of iron from ore, blacksmithing and bronze-casting. The scale of houses and range of crafts mark Birnie out as a central site in the area, and it was well connected: the finds testify to links across the Moray Firth to Sutherland and down the coast to southern Scotland.

This pivotal site drew the attention of the advancing Roman Empire. Such local power centres were exactly the kind of places which the Romans wanted to know about and influence. The range of Roman finds recovered in the excavations suggests that the inhabitants had a long-term relationship with the Roman world, receiving fine pottery and glass vessels, unusual glass beads, exotic brooches, and a remarkable bird-headed pin which may have been a special commission [3.14, 3.15]. The quantities are small but significant, showing long-term links to these northern groups.

It was probably this existing relationship which brought the coins to the site, with the Romans using their hard-won knowledge of local politics to try to influence matters in Moray. Metal-detecting had picked up plough-scattered trails from a hoard which we were able to excavate and lift in a block of soil for study in the lab [3.1, 3.12]. The following year excavations found a second, intact, hoard, just a few metres away [3.13].

These hoards provided remarkable information, not just on the silver coins but also the context of their burial. The coins may have been nominally silver but this had been alloyed with copper, and during the long stay in the soil the copper had

SCOTLAND'S EARLY SILVER

Fig. 3.13: The second, intact, *denarius* hoard, containing 310 coins, the latest of AD 193.

corroded, creating a toxic environment inside the pots which halted the decay of organic materials. Careful conservation work and subsequent specialist analysis revealed some remarkable insights. The coins had been buried in locally-made pots, each containing two batches. This was clearest in the intact hoard, where two finely-made leather bags were still preserved, but there were also remains of a pouch with some coins in the other hoard. Interestingly, analysis showed that this was made of Roman leather – perhaps the original container for the coins on their travels north – while the other bags were Iron Age. The plough-damaged pot had been lined with bracken to cushion those coins not in a pouch, and this had preserved pollen from the atmosphere on the day of burial – providing a snapshot of the environment at the time, and confirming it was a busy farming landscape, with both crops and grazing in the area.

What of the silver? The two hoards were very similar – both contained just over 300 coins (weighing 900 and 1020 grams).[31] The dates of the latest coins (AD 193 and 196) show that they left the Roman world a few years apart. This looks like traces of a pattern of regular payments to the site's occupants. But why bury them? Excavations helped to answer this as well. The hoards were not hidden – they were buried in an open, visible part of the site. Indeed, one of them lay directly outside the door of a house, and it seems both were marked by small posts. There were other unusual deposits nearby – a pit with a quern (a grinding stone for grain) buried upside down, another with an unusual, almost unused whetstone placed on its base. In a further pit, parts of a smashed pot had been deposited along with a range of organic remains. This looks to be deliberate – the traces of ancient rituals. It seems these valued goods were put in a special part of the site as offerings.

Not long after this, around AD 200, the Birnie village was abandoned; the hoards may even have been buried as part of the closing rites on this time-honoured site. It seems this and other long-lived farming settlements were abandoned and traditions changed. Were these upheavals caused by the meddling of the Roman world in local politics?

NOTES

1. Dio Cassius LXXII, 8; translation from Ireland 2008, 103.
2. Commodus sent an expeditionary force north under Ulpius Marcellus, the Governor of Britain, which 'inflicted major defeats on the barbarians' (Dio Cassius LXXII, 8; translation from Ireland 2008, 103; see also Birley 2005, 162–70).
3. See Heather 2017, 24 for this in a 4th-century context: '… the empire was prompted into a really serious – and hence expensive – military campaign on each major sector of its riverine European campaigns … about once per political generation: every twenty years or so.'
4. It was not the only medium. There is evidence of fine tablewares – pottery, and especially glass – being sent north, and some jewellery (Holmes and Hunter 2001). But these were in relatively small numbers and were familiar, whereas silver coinage in this quantity was novel.
5. Hunter 2007a; 2015; Holmes 2014. This tally excludes hoards associated with Roman sites.
6. Lind 1981. Note that there have been many more recent finds, and Lind only plotted discoveries of over 20 coins, but the broad patterns seem to remain valid. For consistency, only finds of over 20 coins from Britain and Ireland are plotted.
7. Epitome of Dio Cassius LXXV, 5, 4; translation from Ireland 2008, 112–13.
8. Approaching motives for burial of hoards is always difficult, but here one can use both general and particular arguments. There was a general Iron Age tradition of burying valued items in special, often wet places; these are best seen as deliberate offerings. In the case of Birnie, the burial of two hoards in the open rather than hidden, both apparently marked by stakes, and in an area which saw other unusual deposits, suggests this was a sacrifice in public view, not intended for recovery.
9. The rarity of single *denarii* and smaller-denomination bronze coins is convincing evidence that they were not used for trade, since monetary exchange requires small change and generates losses as people drop coins in their dealings.
10. A major programme of surface analysis of crucibles by Andrew Heald (2005) found no secure evidence of silver-working until the 4th or 5th centuries AD. This Caledonian desire to preserve silver coins was not shared elsewhere: in much of Germany, coins were readily melted down (Voß 2013; Rau 2013a, 353).
11. There is a parallel with late Roman gold medallions found beyond the continental frontier. These were mounted to display the face of the emperor, which was seen as the important side (Bursche 2001, 89).
12. For a recent survey, see Farley and Hunter (eds) 2015.
13. Stribrny 2003.
14. One mould comes from an Iron Age site at Brighouse Bay in Kirkcudbrightshire, straight across the Solway Firth from coin-using Roman Britain; two from the former Roman fort of Newstead (on the direct road south to the province, but a safe distance beyond official eyes); and one from Dundee (Holmes and Hunter 2001; Holmes 2012, 133). A straightforwardly fraudulent explanation is not entirely convincing owing to numismatic oddities in the coins being made, though the technology involved is exactly the same as one finds within the Roman Empire. Most post-date the main period of *denarius* hoards, further diminishing the likelihood of a connection to local coin use.
15. Watson 1926, 21–2, 58–9; Fraser 2005, 33–5.
16. It is striking that East Lothian has produced no *denarius* hoards, although other evidence suggests that the area was pro-Roman at the time and the central site of Traprain Law has produced a wealth of finds of the period (see pages 41–2). (It does not have coinage of the late 2nd century, so it seems coins were genuinely not present, rather than not hoarded.) It seems different relationships were in play in different areas.
17. Roman coins were stamped with information which allows us to establish their date. A typical hoard will have a few fresh coins, a few old coins, and a lot of coins which have been circulating for 10–20 years. Things are not so dissimilar today, though the introduction of new coins biases matters. For instance, as I write this

Fig. 3.14 (above): Unique copper-alloy bird-shaped pin head from Birnie, Moray; 19 mm (bird length).

Fig. 3.15 (below): Roman brooches from Birnie.

almost half the coins in my pocket come from the current decade, a third are from the previous decade, and the oldest coins date from 1982. There is also at least one fake pound coin and two low-denomination foreign coins. Even if the latest coins were missing, the overall composition would still point to a date in the 2010s.

18. Holmes 2014; Hunter 2015.
19. Hodgson 2014 provides an up-to-date assessment of the campaigns.
20. See translations in Ireland 2008, 114–16.
21. Herodian III, 15, 6–7; translation from Ireland 2008, 119.
22. Braund 1984, 94–9, 165–6.
23. For example, Horsnæs 2010, 98, 129, 135.
24. See Hardt 2015 for recent discussion of Childeric's dates.
25. Martin 2004; Quast 2015b, 179.
26. For the earlier metalwork tradition in the area and aspects of the transition, see Hunter 2014a; for an overview of changes, Hunter 2007b; 2014b.
27. Mann 1974.
28. For example, Ferguson and Whitehead 1999.
29. Breeze 1982, 144–53.
30. Full publication is in progress. The work was directed by Fraser Hunter and funded primarily by National Museums Scotland and Historic Environment Scotland, with additional funding from the Society of Antiquaries of Scotland, Moray Society, Moray Field Club, Ian Keillar, Lord Doune and Cardiff University.
31. For numismatic detail see Holmes 2006, where weights are discussed on p. 20; they are too variable to demonstrate they are clear multiples of a Roman pound (3 pounds would weigh *c.* 970 g).

BRIBERY BEYOND *BRITANNIA*

CHAPTER FOUR
Silver for changing times
AD 250–350

The conservator's workbench was covered in an infernal silver jigsaw. Tiny fragments with curves and dots were carefully cleaned and then checked against the developing picture with endless patience. Most were returned to the unmatched pile, but every so often another join was found, and the picture extended. Slowly, painstakingly, a Roman bowl emerged from the silver shrapnel [Fig. 4.1].

The fragments came from an exciting new find – a hoard of hacked-up Roman silver found at Dairsie in Fife during a metal-detecting rally in 2015. They once formed fine silver vessels which graced a rich Roman's table before they came north. This discovery is changing the way we

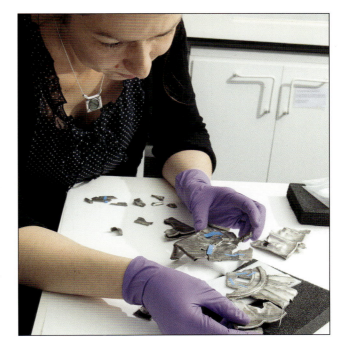

Fig. 4.1 (right): Conservation of the Dairsie hacksilver hoard in progress.

Opposite: Hacked-up Roman silver vessels from Dairsie in Fife; NMS X.FRH 1–2.

Fig. 4.2 (opposite): Roman silver crossbow brooch from Carn Liath, Sutherland; 76mm (length). Dunrobin Museum 1863.7. Image © National Museums Scotland.

think about Roman contacts with Scotland, for they date to a critical, little-known period – the 3rd century AD.

ECONOMIC CRISIS

Hoards of silver coins (*denarii*) came to an end in the early 3rd century AD. The days of the *denarius* were numbered. It had served Rome well since the 3rd century BC, but now the Roman economy was struggling and the emperor needed to make his silver go further.

Initially the *denarius* was diluted, its silver content dropping from around 80% in AD 64 to around 46% in AD 194.[1] Then, in a devious sleight of hand, its successor was introduced to the economy – the double-*denarius* or radiate. Its name might suggest it had twice the silver content, but in practice it was only around one-and-a-half times.[2] This was the beginning of a rapid slide into economic chaos and rampant inflation: within fifty years these coins were made of copper alloy with barely a surface lick of silver, and counterfeiting was rife. In many ways the coins are emblematic of wider problems in the Empire – the orderly succession of emperors broke down, with a series of soldier-emperors seizing power with the armies under their control, sometimes only for a matter of months before their grisly dispatch by the next would-be strongman. Emboldened by the visible frontier turmoil, and perhaps also drawn in by the collapse of their traditional subsidies from Rome, groups beyond the Rhine and Danube began raiding deep into the Gaulish and German provinces.

With successive short-lived emperors more concerned with their own survival than that of the frontiers, some of the border provinces broke away to run themselves. The so-called Gallic Empire, consisting of France and neighbouring areas, was separate from the main Empire for 15 years, from AD 260–74, and its rulers had considerable success in beating back the barbarian tribes who were causing enormous problems at the time. It spawned further separatists – *Britannia* broke away from AD 286–96, the general Carausius who had been leading campaigns against pirates in the English Channel taking matters into his own hands and separating Britain from the main Empire. It was a short-lived sovereignty: he was killed by his own finance minister, Allectus, who in turn was killed when the central Empire re-established control, brought separatists back into the fold and beat enough barbarians to keep the peace.

THE NORTHERN FRONTIER IN THE THIRD CENTURY

In all this turmoil, it seems the northern frontier stayed quiet.[3] As we have seen (page 26), the historical sources are silent on our edge of the Empire. There is no sign of trouble, certainly compared to elsewhere. The combination of silver coin hoards and military interventions in the early 3rd century had quelled the frontier's trouble-spots, more likely by destabilising them than winning them over. But the new hoard from Fife shows that the northern frontier was not forgotten.

There have always been hints of a continuing relationship, though never very clear. The great hillfort of Traprain Law near Haddington, 40 km east of Edinburgh, had a favoured relationship with the Roman world over several

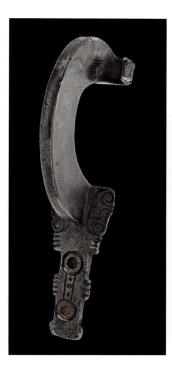

Fig. 4.3 (below): Roman silver finger-ring fragment with gemstone showing Mars and Victory, Capledrae, Fife; 15 mm (height of gem). Fife Cultural Trust Collection. Image © National Museums Scotland.

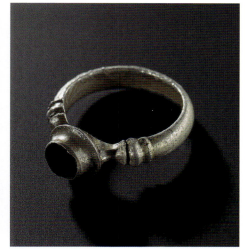

Fig. 4.4 (below): Roman gilt silver ring of 3rd-century date, Culbin Sands, Moray; 24 mm (diameter), NMS X.BI 25639.

hundred years (pp. 41–2). Throughout the 3rd century, Roman finds from the hill provide testament to continuing contacts in pottery, fine glassware, and brooches, as well as low-value copper-alloy coins which suggest direct exchanges with the Roman world.[4] Elsewhere the evidence is sparse, although a few clusters of late Roman coins in southern Scotland point to hotspots of contact with Rome in the later 3rd and 4th centuries. These coins were virtually valueless except in dealings with Rome, and they concentrate at coastal or river locations which make natural meeting places.[5]

But recent research into old and new finds is adding different aspects to our story, and silver played a key role. A silver brooch from Carn Liath broch in Sutherland has long been seen as a local copy of a Roman crossbow-shaped brooch, not least because the design on the foot resembled a simple Pictish symbol [4.2].[6] Yet the form of the brooch finds rare but exact parallels in the Roman world,[7] while analysis confirmed its composition was consistent with Roman silver.[8] This was a Roman brooch, not a local copy.

Its discovery 350 km north of Hadrian's Wall may seem unlikely, but it fits a pattern of occasional Roman links far beyond the frontier. The rarity of intervening finds and often-impressive nature of these northern discoveries suggests direct diplomatic contact from the Roman world rather than items moving from hand to hand up the coast.[9]

Another old discovery has been even more evasive – until recently. An obscure local history book published in 1924 noted that 'some Roman jewellery was found about forty years ago' by 'the Devil's Stane' at Capledrae in Fife, south of Loch Leven.[10] There was no other source for this and no surviving finds, so it had been ignored – old books are full of 'Roman finds' which are nothing of the kind, since 'Roman' was often a default identification for anything old. But this scepticism was misplaced. In 2016, metal-detecting in this very area produced a silver ring with an engraved gemstone of the god Mars holding a statuette of the goddess Victory [4.3]. The style of ring is most typical of the 3rd or 4th century.[11]

Searching for the missing Fife finds in our collections

SILVER FOR CHANGING TIMES

35

Fig. 4.5: Excavating the Dairsie hacksilver hoard. Flags mark where silver fragments were found.

Fig. 4.6: The findspot of the Dairsie hacksilver hoard. In the foreground are pits which once held Bronze Age standing stones; at the rear of the trench, an area of dark soil marks a small peat bog. The silver hoard was buried between the two.

led to another unexpected discovery – a further 3rd-century Roman silver ring, found at Culbin Sands in Moray in the 19th century but long assumed to be Medieval [4.4]. Excavation in the archives is always worthwhile, and these 'new' finds reveal that more silver made its way north than we had thought in the decades after the Romans had pulled back to Hadrian's Wall.

INVESTIGATING THE DAIRSIE HOARD

These hints of a continuing political engagement between parts of Scotland and the Roman world received dramatic confirmation in 2015. The field chosen by Detecting Scotland for their metal-detecting rally had no obvious archaeological significance – there were no known finds from it, but it was good arable land, recently harvested, and the detectorists fanned out to see what they could find. Among the normal harvest of ring-pulls and musket balls, schoolboy David Hall found some more unusual items, of strange shape and colour. Could these be silver? Might they even be Roman? Soon, more and more similar fragments were plucked from the soil. It was a scattered hoard.

The discovery was quickly reported to the Treasure Trove Unit (TTU) and an excavation mounted. Led by archaeologists from the National Museum working with TTU colleagues and some of the detectorists, we plotted where their finds came from to reveal a cluster of fragments. Geophysical survey showed no obvious settlement in the area, but suggested there were a few hidden features.[12] Using a mechanical excavator, we stripped off thin spits of soil in a large area around the silver cluster, in order to recover as many fragments as possible [4.5]. The metal-detectorists found more and more pieces of silver – over

SCOTLAND'S EARLY SILVER

Fig. 4.7 (below): The Roman hacksilver hoard from Dairsie, Fife. National Museums Scotland X.FRH 1–4.

Fig. 4.8 (right, above): Roman dish from the Dairsie hoard. The folded package represents a quarter of the vessel; a second quarter was buried but was heavily damaged by the plough. One fragment shows the decorative design from the centre of the dish; c.360 mm (original diameter), NMS X.FRH 1.

Fig. 4.9 (right, below): Underside of the fluted bowl from the Dairsie hoard. It was first cut in half, each of which was then cut down to a third. These were folded tightly into packages which were broken by the plough; 300 mm (original diameter), NMS X.FRH 2.

SILVER FOR CHANGING TIMES

400 were recovered in total. As the remaining ploughsoil was cleaned away by hand, we began to see the setting of the hoard. The geophysics had spoken true: it was not buried in a settlement, but away from normal domestic activity in an area which would have been memorable, perhaps even sacred [4.6]. The site lies on a terrace above a small river. A few metres to one side of the findspot was a small peat bog – an unusual feature on a terrace, perhaps caused by a spring. Such watery features were often seen as sacred or special places in antiquity. A few metres in the other direction were some postholes and two large pits which contained the stumps of standing stones. These were much older than the hoard – such stones marked sacred places of the Bronze Age, around 2000 BC. This hoard was buried between an unusual wet place and an ancient monument. Was this a recognisable location for later recovery? Or was it buried in this special place as an offering?

This resonates with the jewellery from Capledrae, discussed above, which had been buried by 'the Devil's Stane', an older standing stone, and with two hoards we will meet in chapter 7, from Norrie's Law (also in Fife) and Gaulcross in Aberdeenshire, both buried in older sites. These ancient monuments must have attracted myths and stories. Burying a valuable hoard there was not just a handy hiding place – these would have been special locations for later generations, imbued with the spirits of the ancestors.[13] Such hoards are best seen as offerings.

What of the Dairsie hoard itself? It consists of parts of four vessels [4.7]. One was a dish some 360 mm in diameter with an ornate central design inlaid with niello, a black paste made of silver sulphide which would contrast visually with the silver [4.8]. Its surface was further decorated with lathe-formed lines, while beaded patterns adorned the edge. The second vessel was a fluted basin on a low footring [4.9]. This style of vessel was probably used to wash one's hands at a feast.[14] The third was a globular bowl about 170 mm in diameter with an out-turned rim and an ornate decorative pattern punched into the thin metal from the outside, leaving a raised design visible when the diner looked into the bowl [4.10].[15] It showed a wreath of olive leaves round the rim and vines laden with grapes sprouting from ornate vessels, all very appropriate for a dining vessel. The fourth item was also unusual. It is a thick, irregular disc of silver which has been hammered into a cylinder.

Fig. 4.10: Fragmentary repoussé-decorated bowl from the Dairsie hoard. Below a wreath of olive leaves is a design of roundels alternating with vases from which vines grow, and fragmentary arches; c.165 mm (original diameter), NMS X.FRH 3.

Fig. 4.11 (left): Dish from the silver hoard from Chaourse (Picardy, France) similar to the dish from Dairsie; 330 mm (diameter), British Museum 1889,1019.19.

Fig. 4.12: Fluted bowl from the Chaourse hoard, similar to the one from Dairsie; 240 mm (diameter), British Museum 1890,0923.4.

Fig. 4.13: Beaker from the Chaourse hoard, similar to one from Dairsie; 115 mm (diameter), British Museum 1889,1019.10.

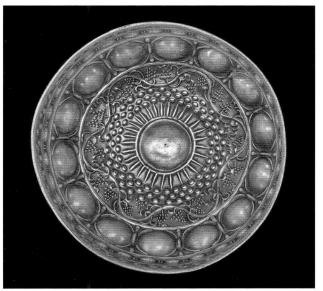

The surface is very rough and uneven from the hammering; it may even have been part of a flawed casting which was used as bullion rather than re-melted or repaired. The styles of the plate, bowl and fluted dish are typical of later 3rd-century vessels, such as those in the Chaourse hoard from northern France [4.11–4.13].[16]

The plough has ripped the Dairsie vessels to pieces, but they had been treated rather brutally already. The small bowl was probably intact when buried, but the disc had been reshaped to a cylinder and both other vessels had been cut up. The platter had been cut in half and then halved again, with only two quarters buried, both folded up into packages. The fluted dish had likewise been chopped in half, with a third of each half removed and the rest folded into a package. The hack-marks from the chisel are still clearly visible.

It is tempting to see this hacking as a barbarian act, carried out beyond the frontier by hoodlums with no respect for Classical art. As we will see in the next chapter, the evidence suggests otherwise. Silver was treated this way within the Roman Empire from at least the 2nd century AD as valuable items were transformed into raw material for reuse. It is most likely the Dairsie find was a ready-hacked

SILVER FOR CHANGING TIMES

Fig. 4.14 (opposite): The hillfort of Traprain Law, from the north.

weight of silver passed north as a subsidy or a gift. This represents a significant shift away from diplomacy in increasingly devalued coin to high-quality bullion. It is the earliest such hacksilver hoard beyond the Roman frontier anywhere in Europe. These plough-shattered fragments so painstakingly pieced back together are vital testaments to shifting Roman frontier policy.

Why did they come to eastern Fife? It seems that powerful leaders here had stayed on good terms with the Roman world. No Roman forts are known in Fife, and even temporary camps from military campaigns are rare. Indeed, the disposition of Roman forts to the north in Perthshire may have been intended in part to screen Fife from antagonistic neighbours.[17] Its residents received large amounts of silver coinage during the phase of diplomatic sweeteners in the late 2nd century, so it is little surprise that more silver was sent north to keep these long-term allies friendly.

But the earlier policy of pay-offs had created problems. In north-east Scotland, Roman sources started to talk of a group called the Picts. There may have been a power-struggle in the area, with anti-Roman factions in society seizing power. The emergence of a few strongly fortified sites at this time suggests the development of powerful but paranoid warlords, seizing and holding control through military strength rather than age-old claims to land or favoured links to the Roman world.[18] Around AD 300 the northern frontier zone was being raided once more, with attacks becoming increasingly audacious – there is evidence of raiding down the Yorkshire coast and deep into the heart of southern England, creating far more troubles than the Romans had seen before.[19] It was the law of unintended consequences: Roman silver diplomacy worked in the short-term in keeping the tribes quiet and then destabilising them, but in the longer term it created a much more dangerous enemy. It shows the unpredictable consequences of interfering in other societies – a point familiar from more recent imperial adventures, such as British and Russian interventions in Afghanistan in the 19th century, or indeed western interventions in the same area today.

How could the Roman world deal with this new problem? Once again they tried their traditional strategies, warfare and diplomacy – and once again, silver was to the fore. The Dairsie hoard is a prelude to the flow of silver northwards from the Roman world in the 4th and 5th centuries.

TRAPRAIN LAW: THE HILL ON THE EMPIRE'S EDGE

Traprain Law is an imposing, elongated volcanic hill which dominates the fertile East Lothian coastal plain [4.14]. The site has attracted people for millennia, with traces of Mesolithic hunter-gatherers, ritual use by Neolithic farmers, and burials in the earlier Bronze Age. In the later Bronze Age (c.1200–800 BC) it became a fortified settlement and local power centre. When this was abandoned, it served as a gathering point for dispersed local communities during the Iron Age.

But for the story of silver the key phase of the site is its relationship with the Roman world. In the 1st century AD a major settlement was established which dominated the local area. This may have been the outcome of competition among local groups, with one taking overall leadership, or it may have been prompted by the threat of the recently-arrived Romans, causing disparate groups to work together. But whoever was leading the people on Traprain worked the politics well – they built up good relations with the Roman world which lasted for several centuries. This is seen in the wealth of Roman finds from the Law [4.15] – fine pottery and glassware, a vast range of brooches, and even a stone with the first letters of the alphabet [4.16], suggesting some people on the site were learning Latin for their dealings with Rome. It is also marked by the absence of Roman military sites anywhere nearby. East Lothian was seen by the Romans as friendly territory and perhaps treated as a client kingdom of Rome, acting as a buffer against potentially hostile groups further north.

Successive generations on Traprain played this game well. Roman material came to the site both at times when other parts of Scotland were occupied by the army and when the frontier lay further south, on Hadrian's Wall. It seems the people on

Traprain were valued allies, pinning their loyalties to Rome's eagle. The great silver Treasure from the site, explored in the next chapter, is among the latest Roman finds from the hill, at a time when the Empire was in turmoil and old loyalties were called on once more. Around this time, in the 5th century AD, a massive fortification wall was built around the hill, testament to these uncertain times – for the rest of the Roman period the site had been unfortified, though its old defences were visible reminders of its ancient history. Occupation did not end with the burying of the great silver hoard; there is evidence of continuing activity through the 5th and into the 6th century, though in the wider power-politics of the time it ultimately lost out to its neighbours, perhaps those under what is now Edinburgh Castle.

Fig. 4.15 (above): Selection of Roman finds from Traprain Law – fine pottery and glass, jewellery, a folding spoon, and a stone inscribed with the beginning of the alphabet, shown on the left (**4.16**); 35 mm (length), NMS X.GV 968.

SCOTLAND'S EARLY SILVER

42

NOTES

1. See Butcher and Ponting 2014, 701 for a summary of their extensive work on late 1st-/early 2nd-century coinage; Butcher and Ponting 2012 for 2nd-century coinage; Gitler and Ponting 2003, 26, fig. 17 for the Severan debasement.
2. The radiate (a modern term derived from the radiate crown worn by the emperor) was introduced briefly by Caracalla in AD 215. It was so unpopular because of its low silver content that it was withdrawn in 222, but then reintroduced in 238 (Casey 1980, 9–11; Moorhead n.d. [2013], 10).
3. Breeze 1982, 144–53.
4. Hunter 2009b.
5. Hunter 2010.
6. Curle 1932, 338; Ritchie 1989, 51; Cessford 1997.
7. It is a rare variant of late Roman crossbow brooch, dating to around AD 300; a full study is in preparation, but note *inter alia* parallels from Serbia, Germany and an unknown findspot (Popović 1996, 193, no. 147; Erdrich 2002, Taf. 4.4; Ogden 1982, fig. 4:77). Several components had been deliberately removed, making identification trickier; arms were once soldered under the head, a rivet hole once held a decorative knob, and the pin holder has been removed. There are no strong grounds for seeing the decoration on the foot as a Pictish symbol (contra Ritchie 1989, 51; Cessford 1997), as the ring-and-dot motifs appear to be an integral part of the casting, though lines could have been added later to create a symbol from two original ring-and-dots. Crossbow brooches were symbols of official service for Rome, especially (but not exclusively) military. Two further Scottish finds of early P-shaped crossbows of 3rd-century date (from Traprain Law and Ardnave, Islay, were made in copper alloy coated in tin to mimic silver (Ritchie and Welfare 1983, 341–3, no. 62; Burley 1956, 162, no. 53).
8. Unpublished analysis by Dr Lore Troalen when the brooch was on loan to National Museums Scotland thanks to the kindness of Lord Strathnaver.
9. A notable cluster of late Roman finds (3rd–4th century AD) in northern Scotland (Hunter 2014b, fig. 2b) includes spectacular items such as a gold crossbow brooch from the Moray Firth area and a bronze vessel hoard from Helmsdale, Sutherland.
10. Houston 1924, 60.
11. Guiraud (1989) type 4c, dated to the late 3rd or 4th century, reusing an older gem (compare related gems from Britain and Carnuntum, Austria; Henig 2007, nos 90–2; Dembski 2005, 68, Taf. 15, no. 151).
12. Survey by Dr Tessa Poller of the University of Glasgow.
13. For later reuse of prehistoric monuments, see papers in Bradley and Williams 1998, especially Williams 1998, Semple 1998 and, in a Scottish context, Driscoll 1998.
14. Hobbs 2016, 187.
15. Such vessels have been studied in detail by Barbara Niemeyer (2004); most are beakers 11–14 cm in diameter with larger ones less likely to be drinking vessels, at least for alcohol. Three of the four British and Irish finds fall into this larger category: Dairsie, Ballinrees (Co. Derry) and Water Newton (Cambridgeshire), the latter a hanging lamp (Niemeyer 2004, Abb. 10). These vessels are known only in the north-west provinces and the 'barbarian' lands beyond, and were probably made in Gaul and Britain.
16. Baratte and Painter (1989) collected many of the parallels in their valuable catalogue. Compare especially the hoard from Chaourse, with examples of all three main vessel types (*ibid.*, cat. nos 58–64, 85). The platter's bead-and-reel decoration can be paralleled in many 3rd-century finds (e.g. *ibid.*, cat. nos 62–4, 67–73, 78–80), as can the fluted dish (e.g. Hobbs 2016, plate 317). For repoussé-decorated bowls see Niemeyer 2004.
17. Hanson and Maxwell 1986, 41, 169.
18. The work of the Northern Picts project at the University of Aberdeen has revealed a number of well-fortified power centres of this period (such as Rhynie and Dunnicaer in Aberdeenshire), markedly different from what went before (Noble et al. 2013; Noble, Goldberg and Hamilton, in preparation).
19. Breeze 1982, 153–9; Ireland 2008, 146–63.

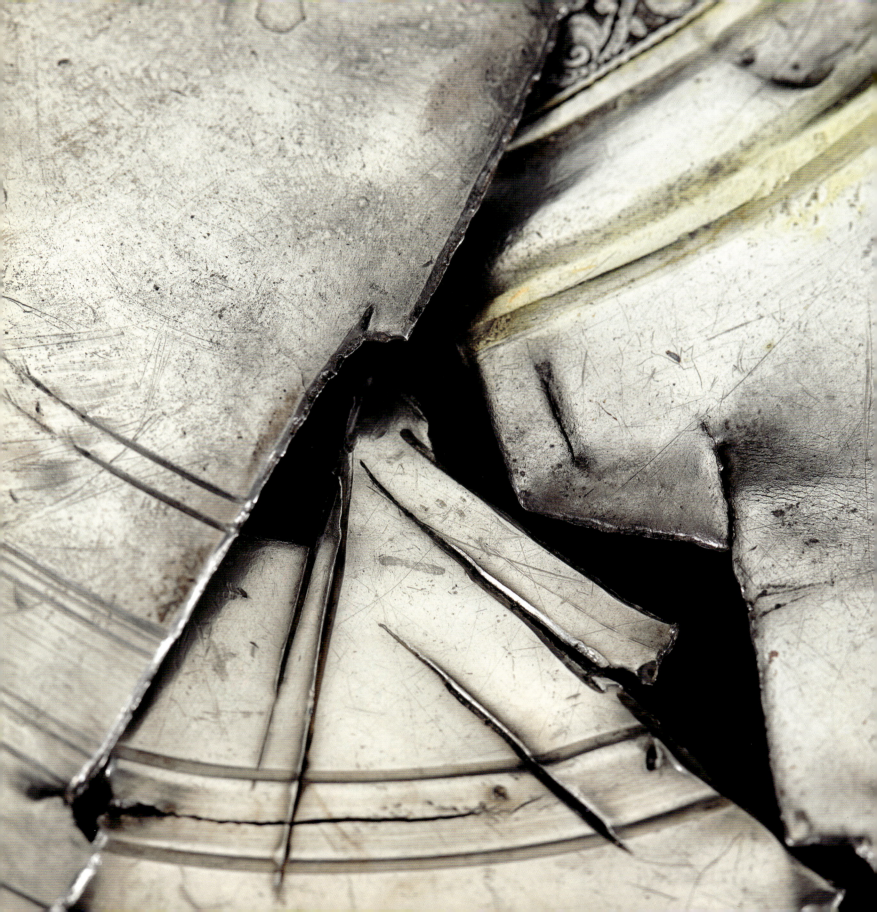

CHAPTER FIVE
Pieces of silver: making sense of the Traprain Treasure
AD 350–450

Imagine my surprise on reaching the site of the digging to see, ranged against the bank at the edge, a great collection of what appeared to be strange, battered & broken vessels of silver, much tarnished though in places still bright, and even in places gilded.[1]

This is how Alexander Curle, who led the excavations at Traprain Law in East Lothian (pp. 41–2), recorded his first impressions of this famous silver hoard in his diary.

The silver was discovered on 12 May 1919. As was normal at the time, the director visited the site only every few days, leaving the daily conduct of the digging to workmen under an experienced foreman. They recognised the

Fig. 5.1 (right): The Traprain Treasure, photographed by Alexander Curle the day after its discovery.

Opposite: Pieces of hacked silver from Traprain Law, East Lothian.

PIECES OF SILVER

45

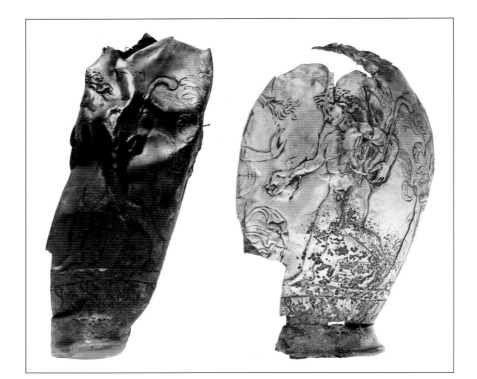

Fig. 5.2: Flagon showing a satyr pursuing a nymph, before (left) and after restoration (right), Traprain Law, East Lothian; 160mm (height), NMS X.GVA 7.

significance of the discovery, and telephoned Curle at the National Museum of Antiquities of Scotland, where he was director,[2] but the message they left was so guarded he did not at first realise the find's significance. He visited the following afternoon and was astounded by what he saw [Fig. 5.1]. Nothing like this had ever been found in Scotland, and it was instantly clear it was of European importance. To this day, the Traprain Treasure has an international reputation.

The finds were not in great condition after their long burial, and it took a lot of fairly brutal restoration work to get them to their current display condition. The work was not done by Museum conservators but professional silversmiths, Brook and Son on George Street in Edinburgh. The firm's owners had been involved with the Museum for many years, and with their craft skills they were an obvious choice for such specialist work.

The decayed silver was heated repeatedly, plunged in acid baths and hammered back into shape – techniques that make modern curators wince [5.2].[3] Missing parts were restored, packages of silver were unfolded, damaged gilding replaced, and the whole hoard left in a shiny, impressive condition. Brook and Son also made replicas and reconstructions for sale, which proved highly popular (pages 63–4).

Even with this extreme conservation, the fragmentary condition of the material is obvious. This hoard of over 23 kilograms of Roman silver went into the ground in pieces. But before we explore the reasons for this, it is worth looking at what the contents once represented [5.3].

SILVER SERVICE: ÉLITE LIFESTYLES IN THE LATE ROMAN WORLD

The Traprain hoard is dominated by fragments of tableware – plates, bowls, jugs and basins [5.4], and some highly unusual pieces such as a unique triangular bowl, a heart-shaped fish dish [5.5] and a silver framework for a glass

Fig. 5.3: The Traprain Treasure. This image, specially taken for this publication, is the first time the whole hoard has been photographed since 1919; NMS X.GVA 1–176.

Fig. 5.4 (above, left): Tableware from the Traprain Law Treasure, East Lothian.

Fig. 5.5 (above, right): Hacked-up fish dish from Traprain Law, originally heart-shaped; 166 mm (length), NMS X.GVA 108.

Fig. 5.6a (below, left): Fragments from the rim of a large dish from Traprain Law; 98 mm and 86 mm (lengths), NMS X.GVA 63.

Fig. 5.6b (below, right): Reconstruction of the original dish, from Traprain Law; *c.*70 cm (diameter). Prepared by Relicarte for National Museums Scotland.

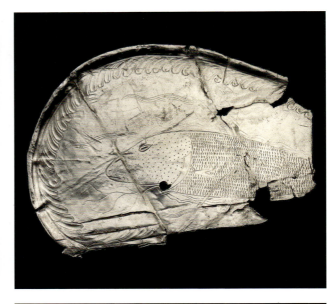

SCOTLAND'S EARLY SILVER

48

Fig. 5.7 (left): Fluted dish showing a Nereid (a sea-nymph) riding a sea-panther. The dish was folded in half when discovered. From Traprain Law; 300 mm (diameter), NMS X.GVA 30.

Fig. 5.8 (below): Spoons, ladles and strainers from the Traprain Treasure; NMS X.GVA 97–106.

bucket.[4] These vessels let us glimpse the world of the late Roman élite, where such silver would have graced fine town houses or well-presented villas. At a dinner party, food was served on large platters. The scale of these is difficult to imagine from our fragments, but reconstruction of one, surviving only as two pieces of rim, shows that it was once 70 cm in diameter – one of the largest dishes known from the late Roman world [5.6 a, b]. Its rim bears finely-engraved decoration emphasised by a dark inlay of niello (silver sulphide) and overlaid with gold, drawing the eye to the delicate geometric patterns, curling vegetation and carefully engraved human busts. Individual diners had small plates and bowls, with fluted basins available to wash one's hands at the table – a very necessary facility when food was mostly eaten by hand [5.7]. Silver spoons were also employed, some showing wear from extended use [5.8].

The function of some vessels remains puzzling. A series of cups on long stems with large flat disc-feet look like goblets [5.9], but this has been questioned: similar examples from other hoards are ill-suited to drinking, as their highly ornate rims would be very impractical.[5] Instead, they were multifunctional serving vessels, the base acting as a platter if inverted; gilding on the interior of the 'cup' may have been intended to prevent salty foods from corroding the silver.

Silver cups may be absent, but drinking customs are seen in other ways – notably a series of jugs used for water and wine. The most complete is decorated with biblical scenes from the Old and New Testaments – the temptation of Adam and Eve, Moses striking the Rock of Horeb to bring forth water for the Israelites, the Three Wise Men greeting the Christ-child, and a fourth, damaged scene [5.10].[6] Christian imagery is found on other items – *Chi-Rho* crosses and fish symbols (an ancient Christian

PIECES OF SILVER

Fig. 5.9 (left): 'Goblets' from the Traprain Treasure, one inverted to act as a serving platter; 105mm (height), NMS X.GVA 13–17.

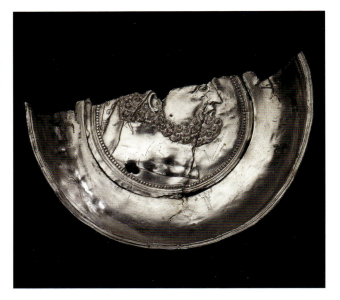

Fig. 5.11 (below): Dish decorated with the face of Hercules, his club behind his head, from Traprain Law; 254 mm (diameter), NMS X.GVA 36.

emblem) on spoons, the letters Alpha and Omega on a belt-fitting. These are the oldest Christian items known from Scotland, but this was no Christian hoard. Other vessels bear figures straight from Roman and Greek myths: Hercules with his club [5.11], a satyr pursuing a nymph with lascivious intent [5.2], a scene from *The Odyssey*. The hoard is strikingly varied.

Although tableware makes up the bulk of the fragments, there is also silver for care of the body. Lidded cylindrical containers once held perfumes and ointments; a mirror lacks only its handle and a final polish to resume its original function; a toothpick points to the Roman élite's

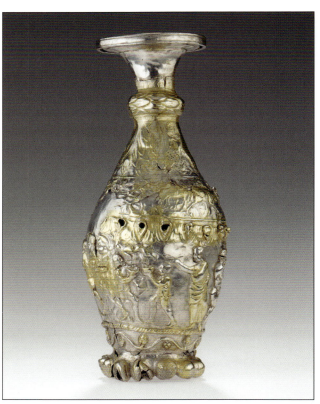

Fig. 5.10 (left): Wine flagon decorated with Old and New Testament scenes. This scene shows Moses striking the Rock of Horeb; Traprain Law, 220mm (height), NMS X.GVA 1.

SCOTLAND'S EARLY SILVER

50

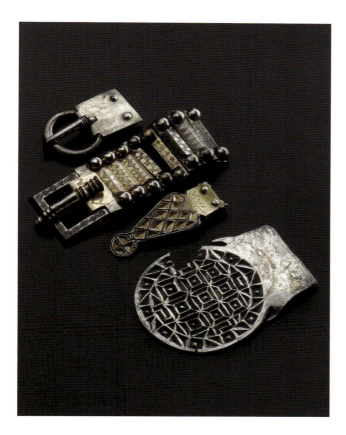

Fig. 5.12: Belt buckles and strap ends from the Traprain Treasure; 75mm (length of front item), NMS X.GVA 146, 147, 149, 150.

concern with personal appearance. There is other personal material: a small brooch and fittings from military belts, the only military material in this frontier hoard [5.12].[7]

But the collection lacks any functional coherence. Other rich treasures of the period consist of dining sets, with matching groups of plates, dishes and so forth.[8] Traprain is a mixture of many different sets. For instance, a normal dinner service would have a single fluted basin for hand-washing, but Traprain has pieces of six; while graffiti carved on the undersides of plates and spoons name at least 18 different owners, not the single name expected with a household's set. The Traprain Treasure was pulled together from a multitude of different sources. Why the mixture?

APPROACHING HACKSILVER

This brings us to the whole question of the nature of hacked-up silver.[9] When the Traprain Treasure was found the interpretation seemed obvious. Only barbarians would treat fine Classical art in this way – it had to be loot. Yet this seems a little strange when the people on this very hilltop had maintained good relations with the Roman world for several hundred years (pp. 41–2). Had things really turned so sour? The hill is rich in other late Roman finds such as fine glassware, suggesting relations were still going strong.[10]

When it was found, the Treasure was virtually unique – there were very few similar finds to compare it with, all much smaller and poorly published.[11] Over the following decades scholars became aware of comparable hoards and raised doubts over the interpretation of the Traprain find.[12] Recent years have seen a flood of new hacksilver hoards from metal-detecting, and National Museums Scotland has been leading a project to re-examine the Traprain Treasure in light of this new evidence.[13] It is now clear that chopping up silver was a regular practice both inside and outside the Roman world from the 2nd century AD onwards, with a strong peak in the 4th and 5th centuries AD [5.13].[14]

So hacking silver was not simply a 'barbarian habit' – it was a practice of the Roman world, particularly in the north-western provinces of the Empire. It was a response to economic needs, with valuable silver converted from artefacts to bullion. The silver may have been beautifully crafted, but its real value was as raw material. The basis of this interpretation is two-fold: the repeated evidence for careful division, not just random chopping [5.14];[15] and subdivision into Roman weight units. This is clearest

PIECES OF SILVER

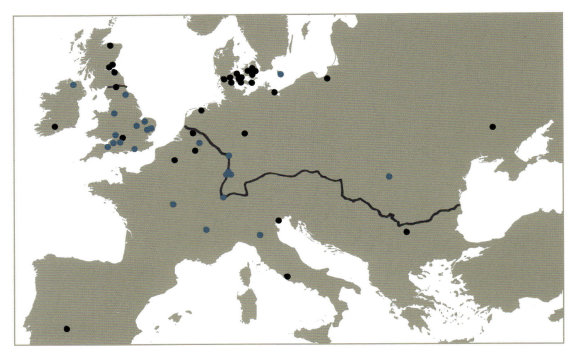

when a single fragment correlates closely to a Roman weight – for instance, a hoard from Water Newton (Cambridgeshire) contained two packets of folded silver weighing one and two pounds respectively.[16] But it is seen in other ways, too. Sometimes an entire cache of silver was collected to make up a particular weight: for example, a handful of silver clippings found with a hoard of gold and silver coins at Patching, Sussex, weighed a pound; while a small group of hacksilver found with gold coins at Echt in the Netherlands weighed half a pound [5.15].[17]

The Traprain evidence is less clear because of its modern history of restoration, but suggestive hints remain. The total surviving weight of the hoard is just over 23.3 kg (close to 71 Roman pounds), but this is unreliable as modern

SCOTLAND'S EARLY SILVER

Fig. 5.13 (opposite): Distribution of Roman hoards including hacksilver. Black symbols are those dominated by hacksilver; blue symbols show where it is a minor element. The lines indicate the Late Roman frontier.

Fig. 5.14 (opposite, below, right): Neatly-cut dish fragment from Traprain Law; 75 mm (radius), NMS X.GVA 38 a.

Fig. 5.15 (opposite, below, left): Hoard of gold coins and hacksilver from Echt (Limburg, Netherlands). Courtesy Vrije Universiteit, Amsterdam.

silver was added to the items in 1919–20. If we look only at unreconstructed pieces, there are clear clusters around multiples of Roman ounces. However, while some items correlate well with Roman standards, others do not.[18] Perhaps these latter were part of a bundle of silver, making up a particular weight – or perhaps they were subdivided later, beyond the frontier, where meeting Roman weight standards was less significant. Certainly, some of the Traprain items show traces of more than one phase of hacking; and as we will see in chapter 7, the cutting-up of silver had an ongoing history in Scotland. But sometimes the fragments give a clearer story. A good example is the two pieces of rim we met earlier which are clearly from the one dish [5.6 a]. Individually their weights show no link to Roman standards, but when added together they weigh almost exactly eight Roman ounces.[19] This was no accident.

So there is good evidence that the cutting up of silver was a Roman economic habit, driven by the core value of silver as raw material rather than a beautiful artefact. What made someone cut up their silver in any particular case is unclear, but overall the habit correlates with times of crisis or economic uncertainty. The 3rd and 4th centuries saw periods of rampant inflation, frontier insecurity and rapidly-changing politics. In uncertain times, people often keep their wealth in portable precious metals – the rising price of gold and silver following the economic crash of 2008 reminds us that this habit is still with us. The prevalence of hacksilver in the later Roman period is thus no surprise.

At certain times there were very particular motives for creating hacksilver. These centuries were full of ambitious men, would-be emperors who needed to buy loyalty from their troops. A potential usurper was at a disadvantage as he lacked control of the imperial treasury. One response was to gather in silver coins and vessels from the areas he controlled in an emergency tax and convert it to bullion, whether as ingots or as hacksilver: the usurper Magnus Maximus, commander of the army of Britain, did exactly this to fund his assault on the throne in AD 383:[20]

> … the money everywhere should be counted, the treasuries should be refilled, coins should be accumulated, and vessels should be broken up.

Thus did silver become hacksilver.

But why did a usurper need silver? Because troops expected to be paid in silver – and gold. Soldiers were kept sweet with precious metal. Rather than the regular and frequent payments of the early Empire, they now received so-called 'donatives' from the emperor on his accession and at regular intervals thereafter [5.16]. For the ordinary soldier this would typically involve five gold coins (*solidi*) and a pound of silver as an accession donative and a further five *solidi* every five years.[21] Those of higher rank might expect silver vessels as containers for the gold, silver military equipment, and perhaps gifts of specially commissioned gold jewellery such as rings or brooches with an inscription of loyalty to the emperor.[22]

So hacksilver represented a response to economic stress, and some cases may be linked to military pay. It was not a barbarian habit in origin, but a Roman one. However, there were differences either side of the frontier. Hacksilver worked within a wider economic system in the Roman world, where silver was also valued for its function as tableware, jewellery or coinage; in hoards inside the Empire,

PIECES OF SILVER

Fig. 5.16: Insignia of the Count of the Sacred Largesse, the *comes sacrarum largitionum*, from the *Notitia Dignitatum*, showing donatives of gold coins in silver vessels surrounded by various silver objects. A detail from a 15th-century copy taken from a 10th-century copy of the original of *c.*AD 400 (see Alexander 1976). Bayerisches Staatsbibliothek München, Clm 10291, fol. 100R.

hacksilver was typically a small component among intact items. But step beyond the frontier and the hacksilver became dominant in hoards [5.13]. These were not caches of precious items, but hoards of bullion.

Opinions differ on what took hacksilver beyond the frontier. Some scholars see loot as the main motive. The classic case is the so-called 'Barbarian Treasure' found in the River Rhine at Neupotz in Germany.[23] Among this massive collection of material, mostly of iron and bronze, is a small amount of hacked silver. Its weights correlate very well with Roman standards, suggesting the hacking was done in the Roman world,[24] but there is little argument that it was part of a large quantity of loot taken from Gaul by Germanic raiders.

Yet looting is a weak explanation for the bulk of hacksilver finds; details of the spatial distribution and the nature of the material suggest other factors were at play. Two other motives are likely. One is the same as in the Roman world – paying soldiers. The late Roman army relied heavily on soldiers recruited from beyond its frontiers, either as individuals or as war bands.[25] At the end of a term of service they would expect to return home with silver and gold in their pouches. Some hoards make good sense as military pay packets, notably Dutch and German finds such as Echt or Großbodungen with a mixture of gold coins and hacksilver [5.15, 5.17]. Gold coins were the normal military pay at this time, hacksilver its supplement; in the case of the Großbodungen hoard the silver came from a special presentation dish gifted by the emperor which was then carefully subdivided, suggesting the division of payment among a war band.[26]

The payment of warriors is a plausible explanation for the Traprain Treasure; pieces of military equipment from the site suggest that some of its inhabitants served in the late Roman army.[27] But it could also be a continuation of the old habit of diplomatic subsidies. The people on Traprain had benefited from friendly connections with Rome for centuries and this silver may be the final fling of a long-lasting relationship. Diplomacy certainly makes sense for some other finds. If one looks at the overall map of hacksilver [5.13], there is a striking difference between Britain, Ireland and the continent. On the islands, hacksilver is found both close to the frontier and in more distant areas; on the continent, there is very little close to the border but a strong concentration in Denmark, 500 km from the Empire's edge. Other evidence indicates that Danish warriors had little to do with the late Roman army – there is very little late Roman military equipment from the area.[28] Instead, these distant contacts are much more likely to represent diplomatic efforts.

So, with Traprain and similar hoards, we can see different processes taking place around the late Roman world: responses to economic challenges which led to the creation of hacksilver, and then military payments, diplomatic

SCOTLAND'S EARLY SILVER

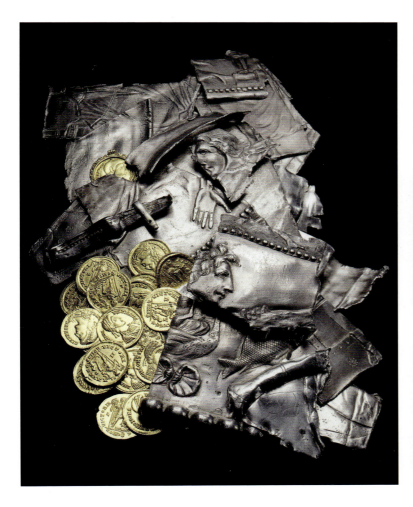

Fig. 5.17 (left): Find of gold coins and hacksilver from Großbodungen, Thuringia, Germany. Landesamt für Denkmalpflege und Archäologie Sachsen-Anhalt, Juraj Lipták.

Fig. 5.18 (below): Gold coin (*solidus*) of Valens (AD 364–7), found by the River Teviot near Jedburgh. The clipping of the edges looks random on the head side, but was intended to make the standing figure on the rear look symmetrical. Probably an early Christian amulet, with the figure of the emperor on the rear interpreted as that of Christ; 18.5 mm (height), NMS X.2001.2.

pay-offs, and raiding (or, more charitably, a self-help mentality) taking it northwards. But Traprain and the other British and Irish hoards are unusual because they are purely silver. On the continent, and indeed in normal payments in the late Roman army, one would have expected gold on top of this. Why the difference?

GOLD AND SILVER

The late Roman state economy relied on gold. Soldiers at this time were paid in gold coins. Gold was also a favoured material for dealing with threatening barbarians. We see this from the history books, with references to eye-watering amounts of gold being paid to barbarian groups. For instance, when Attila the Hun was in his heyday and posing an existential threat to the Roman world, annual payments to him increased from 350 Roman pounds (115 kg) of gold in AD 430 to 700 pounds in AD 437, and 2100 pounds in AD 447 at the height of his power – plus an additional one-off payment of over 6000 pounds that year. After his death, annual payments dropped to a 'mere' 100 pounds.[29] Such payments/pay-offs were viewed differently by different sides: the late Roman bureaucracy gave Attila an army rank and rationalised this as army pay, while to him it was tribute from a weaker foe.[30]

PIECES OF SILVER

55

Fig. 5.19: Medallion of Constantine II Caesar (AD 318), mounted for suspension; the other side is plain. From Birrens, Dumfriesshire; 22 mm (diameter), NMS H.C262.

Fig. 5.20: Fragmentary gold brooch from Erickstanebrae, Dumfriesshire. The openwork inscription running over both faces commemorates twenty years of the Emperor Diocletian's reign on 20 November 303. The inscription reads, 'IOVI AVG / VOT XX' ['Gift of Jovian Augustus, vows for twenty years'] (Collingwood et al. 1991c, 10, 2421.43). The brooch once had a cross-bar similar to Fig. 5.22; 100 mm (length of brooch). Los Angeles County Museum. Image © Museum Associates / LACMA.

Elsewhere archaeology fills in evidence where history is sparse: for instance, the wealth of gold in the lower Rhine area in the early 5th century indicates a targeted policy of gifts to bring the Franks under control.[31] We see its legacy in the wealth of gold in certain areas in the post-Roman period, such as southern Scandinavia, Hungary and Romania.[32] (Jewellery and fittings of silver in these areas confirm it too played a status role on the continent.)[33] And we see it also in surviving diplomatic gifts, such as Roman medallions made for barbarian leaders.[34] But we see very little gold in Scotland and Ireland.

Only three late Roman gold coins are known from Scotland: two from Aberdeenshire, one from the Borders [5.18].[35] They are also rare in Ireland, with ten examples, almost all ritual offerings at the ancient site of Newgrange[36] – in contrast to 2400 known from the lower Rhine (representing 11 kg of gold) around this time.[37] On the continent, large Roman gold medallions circulated as prestige gifts, often mounted for use as ornaments – 35 findspots with over 100 medallions in total are known beyond the Rhine and Danube frontiers, with notable clusters in Denmark, Poland/Ukraine, and Romania.[38] None of these is known from Scotland or Ireland, only smaller single-faced medallions – one from Birrens, Dumfriesshire [5.19], and three from Ireland.[39]

The Birrens medallion is intriguing as it forms part of a small cluster of gold finds in a restricted area of eastern Dumfriesshire. A gold brooch with openwork decoration is known from Erickstanebrae, near Moffat, its inscription marking it out as a gift from the Emperor Diocletian [5.20];[40] while an unusual gold armlet stamped with a Roman inscription is known from Cove, near Ecclefechan [5.21].[41] Such a cluster of prestige material in a small area suggests targeted diplomatic efforts to secure this strategically important area just beyond Hadrian's Wall.[42]

SCOTLAND'S EARLY SILVER

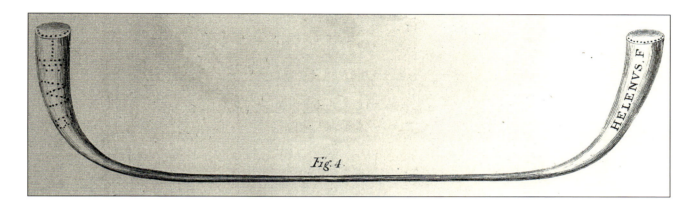

Fig. 5.21: Inscribed late Roman gold armlet (now lost), found around 1750 at Cove, Ecclefechan, Dumfriesshire; c.190mm (length). Image from Pococke 1773, pl. III, fig. 4.

Late Roman gold is otherwise vanishingly rare in Scotland. There is a brooch from the Moray Firth area, its crossbow form a typical marker of late Roman official or military status; this suggests either diplomatic efforts or someone who had ties to the late Roman world [5.22].[43] From Philiphaugh, near Selkirk in the Borders, comes a 4th-century gem-set ring with openwork decoration [5.23].[44] This determined trawl through museum stores and archival references produces only a thin scatter of late Roman gold, in marked contrast to the situation beyond the continental frontier. Some gold was in circulation, but it lacked the staying power of silver.

In contrast to areas such as Denmark, the lower Rhine or Romania,[45] there was no Scottish tradition of locally-made gold jewellery which consumed Roman coinage. Yet there was an abundance of silver – attested not just by surviving hoards such as Traprain but by the amount of silver jewellery from the following centuries, as we shall see.[46] Silver, not gold, was the prestige metal for Scotland. Was this by choice or necessity? Did Roman policy mean there was little gold in circulation, or was silver specifically selected? The answer seems to be a balance between the two. It is clear that much less gold was used for pay-offs in Scotland and Ireland compared to continental frontiers (there was plenty of 4th-century gold coinage within *Britannia*, so the problem was not one of supply to the island).[47] This is likely to reflect the level of perceived threat: while historical sources bemoaned attacks from Scotland and Ireland, it was as nothing compared to the inroads of the Goths or the attacks of the Huns which threatened the very existence of the Empire. Beyond the continental frontier was an enormous land mass with an endless reservoir of potentially hostile groups, while Scotland and Ireland were islands bounded by sea, with limits to the warriors they could support. The marked differential in gold levels suggests a deliberate decision was made to use more silver than gold in dealings with British and Irish barbarians.

Some gold did flow north of Hadrian's Wall, targeted to particular areas of southern and north-east Scotland – eastern Dumfriesshire, the central Borders, Aberdeenshire and the Moray Firth. But while it may have had a short-term significance to its recipients, its long-term impact was limited. This suggests that choice as well as availability played a key role – people preferred silver. Why was this?

Fig. 5.22: Late Roman gold crossbow brooch from the Moray Firth; 79 mm (length), British Museum 1962,1205.1.

Fig. 5.23: Late Roman gold ring from Philiphaugh, Selkirk, Scottish Borders. The gem shows the goddess Ceres; 15 mm (diameter), NMS X.1992.8.

Here we are in the realms of informed speculation. Was there a predisposition to silver because of earlier dealings with Rome and the flow of *denarii* into 2nd-century Scotland? As we have seen, silver was a new metal brought in by Rome – did this give it a continuing significance? Gold had a longer history, stretching intermittently back to the Bronze Age.[48] It was a locally available material, in theory at least, though always rare, and there is little sign of its use in Scotland after the 1st century BC. Perhaps it lacked the exoticness of silver; or perhaps groups in Scotland deliberately chose silver to make a contrast with other cultural groups who preferred gold. We should also be wary of projecting our own value judgements: gold may be the 'gold standard' of value now, but there is ample evidence from other cultures of different choices, and of symbolic meaning behind different metals. For instance, among the Aztecs gold symbolised the sun and silver the moon.[49] There are also signs of a wider British preference for silver in the 4th century: while gold coins were plentiful as single finds in *Britannia*, coin hoards were predominantly silver rather than gold, a reversal of the pattern elsewhere in the Empire.[50]

Such speculations offer a ripe area for further research. What we can say with confidence is that silver became the preferred display metal in Scotland in the Early Medieval period thanks to the wealth of it coming north. Little of this Roman silver now survives – Traprain is exceptional – because so much of it went into the melting-pot. We can see stages of this process in the Traprain hoard, which includes a few small packages of folded plain silver ready for the crucible, while a single dribble of melted silver confirms its intended fate [5.24].

Fig. 5.24: Folded pieces of silver and a melted dribble, from Traprain Law; 30mm (length of melted dribble), NMS X.GVA 142–3.

PLAYING OUT THE ENDGAME OF ROMAN BRITAIN

One final area of the Traprain Treasure merits discussion. We have talked of gifts from the Roman world – but where were they coming from? The hoard offers some rather unexpected clues from its smallest contents – four tiny Roman coins known as *siliquae* [5.25]. These are critical to dating the Treasure and understanding its context. Other components of the hoard can be dated by their style: it includes pieces made at different dates, from around AD 300 to the early 5th century.[51] The coins can be dated quite precisely, the latest being struck for the Emperor Honorius in Milan in AD 397–402.[52] But they tell us more than this. Their current condition is not how they left the mint – they should be much bigger, with a full inscription surrounding the bust of the emperor. They have been clipped – small amounts of silver have been removed around the edge, taking care to preserve the emperor's portrait.

At first sight this looks fraudulent – people removing trimmings which cumulatively would allow them to make something else while the coins still passed in circulation. Such clipping is found in other periods, and was often severely punished by the state if the culprits could be found. Yet research suggests a different story here. Coins were vital to the late Roman economy, but in a frontier province like Britain their supply was not always certain, especially at times of trouble. In the later 4th century, copies of these coins were widely made in good-quality silver, suggesting local enterprise to fill a gap in supply rather than attempts to defraud.[53] In the 5th century the problem got worse. The commander of the British field army drained troops from Britain in AD 407 for his bid to become emperor, leaving behind only the soldiers stationed on the frontiers: he succeeded, temporarily, becoming Constantine III, but was defeated in AD 411. Britain's links to the rest of the Empire collapsed soon after his departure, with virtually no fresh coins reaching Britain after AD 407.[54]

The best interpretation of these clipped *siliquae* is as a response to this lack. They consistently show this pattern of careful clipping, increasingly extreme as time went on and supplies tightened more and more, but always preserving the bust of the emperor, the 'face value' that guaranteed their worth [5.26]. This was probably co-ordinated by the remaining Roman-inspired authorities in southern Britain in an attempt to keep the monetary economy going, with fresh coins made from the clippings. The distribution of clipped *siliquae* shows this was a phenomenon of the east and south of England, not the frontier zones where coin use had been abandoned by now [5.27]. Dating this phenomenon is tricky, but it is best placed in the first half of the 5th century.[55]

This gives us a fascinating context for the Traprain

PIECES OF SILVER

59

Fig. 5.25 (below, left): Silver coins, *siliquae*, of Valens, Eugenius, Arcadius and Honorius from the Traprain Treasure; 15 mm (typical diameter), NMS X.GVA 152 A–D.

Fig. 5.26 (above): The progressive clipping of *siliquae*, from no clipping (left) to heavily-clipped (right). These examples come from various findspots; 18 mm (diameter of coin on left).

Fig. 5.27 (below, right): Distribution of clipped *siliquae* in Britain based on metal-detecting finds (from Bland, Moorhead and Walton 2013, illus. 10.6, with Scottish data added).

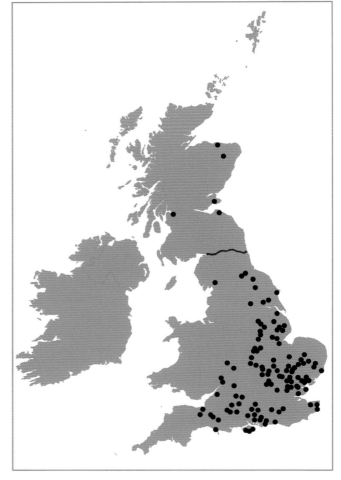

Treasure. It suggests the hacksilver (or at least part of it) came to the site after the formal 'end' of Roman Britain, when it was no longer under direct control of the Empire but some groups in the south were trying to preserve Roman ways of life, and were using silver in the traditional fashion to buy troops or loyalty. The people on Traprain happily accepted this, but the balance of power was changing. The threat of a Roman field army descending on unruly tribes had gone. Power-politics were now smaller scale and more evenly balanced. The threatening hand of Rome was no longer around to crush dissent, but the silver legacy of the Roman world became critical to new power-brokers in the centuries ahead.

Fig. 5.28: X-rays show how this bowl was constructed. The metal is thicker where it is lighter, and thinner where it is darker.

Fig. 5.29 a–c (below, from left): (a) Detail of punched decoration; (b) gilding and niello decoration; (c) a sharp blade cut is visible through one of the beads on the edge of a dish.

SCIENTIFIC ANALYSIS OF THE TRAPRAIN TREASURE

Lore Troalen and Janet Lang

Scientific analysis carried out at National Museums Scotland has given new technical insights into our important collection of Roman silver from Traprain Law. This research has used a broad combination of techniques, including X-radiography, examination with optical microscopes, X-ray fluorescence analysis (see page 7), and scanning electron microscopy (SEM-EDS), which can achieve a high level of magnification combined with detailed analysis of metal composition.

Our investigation of this hoard revealed that the objects were generally made by casting an ingot of the correct approximate shape and then extensively working it to the final form. X-radiography of a bowl [5.28] reveals variations in thickness, seen in regular density differences on the X-ray which arise when the metal has been thinned and shaped by hammering. It also shows small indentations and concentric chased lines which tell us that it has been finished off by turning on a lathe.[56]

Roman silver objects were decorated using a range of techniques: repoussé (relief raised mainly from the back), raising from the front, chasing and punching [5.29a], with colour contrast

obtained by inlaying with niello (a paste of silver sulphide) and coating areas with gold [5.29b].[57] Gilding can be achieved mechanically, using very thinly beaten gold leaf burnished onto the surface; by diffusion bonding, where heat ensured the adhesion of gold foil; or by fire gilding, where an amalgam of gold and mercury was heated, evaporating the mercury and leaving a chemically-bonded coating of gold behind. This last method seems to be the one most commonly used by the Romans.

PIECES OF SILVER

61

 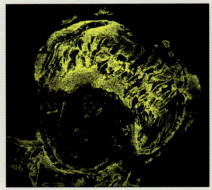 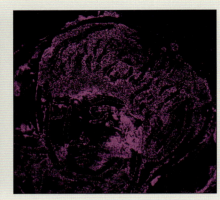

Investigation of a flagon in the scanning electron microscope revealed the use of fire gilding – chemical mapping shows the distribution of mercury as well as gold on the surface of the object [5.30].

Another important element of decoration on Roman silver was the use of beading on the edge of bowls and dishes. Beading was achieved by using a ball-ended punch and a die with a hemispherical cavity in the end.[58] The mark of the edge of the die used to create beading can often be seen under the microscope [5.29 c].

Most of the Traprain Treasure was hacked into pieces. Our microscopic observations revealed the use of several tools to break up the silver, including shears, chisels and other bladed tools such as axes [5.29 c].

Fig. 5.30 (above): Mapping the distribution of different elements over this human portrait (from flagon NMS X.GVA 4) shows where the silver was visible (left, blue), where the gilding was applied (centre, yellow), and where there are traces of mercury from the gilding process (right, pink). The mercury extended beyond the gold – it seems some areas were coated by accident.

Fig. 5.31 (right): Detail of a similar human bust on this flagon from Traprain; NMS X.GVA 4.

MAKING THE MOST OF THE TREASURE: REPLICAS AND SOUVENIRS

The discovery of the Traprain Treasure sparked enormous public interest, with exhibitions, lectures, articles in newspapers and magazines – it even featured on a set of advertising cards for Churchman's Cigarettes [5.33].[59] This interest was fuelled by the silversmiths, Brook and Son, who carried out the restoration work. They saw the commercial possibilities of the find and got permission from the Society of Antiquaries of Scotland (who had funded the excavations) to make replicas of the most intact pieces and reconstructions of the more damaged items, for a suitable commission [5.32]. The small triangular dish was a

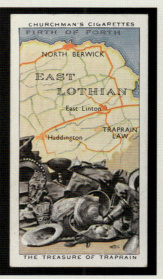

Fig. 5.32 (above): Selection of replicas and reconstructions of the Traprain Treasure, made by Brook and Son.

Fig. 5.33 (right): The Traprain Treasure as shown on Churchman cigarette cards of 1937.

PIECES OF SILVER

63

Fig. 5.34: Condiment set comprising miniature version of Traprain Law vessels, modified for this new function.

Fig. 5.35 a, b: Replica fluted dish presented to A O Curle by the silversmith, William Brook. Below is a detail of the inscription on the base. By courtesy of the family of A O Curle.

favourite, as were the smaller beaded-rim bowls and sets of spoons [5.36], but larger items were also replicated, including the fluted dish with the sea-nymph.

The replicas proved very popular as gifts for society weddings and other presentations. For instance, Alexander Curle, the excavator of Traprain, was given a replica fluted bowl by William Brook [5.35]. Brook and Son also modified Roman forms for modern tastes – the dolphin ladle was pierced to act as a tea strainer, while condiment sets used miniature modified versions of the triangular and beaded bowls, with a flagon repurposed to act as a pepper pot [5.34].

These replicas still turn up in antique shops and auctions today, and are valued collectors' items – though the auctioneers do not always realise what they have. One eminent London auction house (who should remain nameless to save embarrassment) once advertised a Traprain replica dish as a 'haggis platter'!

SCOTLAND'S EARLY SILVER

NOTES

1. From the diary of A O Curle, p. 56.
2. Curle was director of the Royal Scottish Museum on Chambers Street in Edinburgh from 1916–31, following his directorship of the National Museum of Antiquities of Scotland from 1913–19 (he held the two posts together for a few years). These two institutions are the building blocks of the current National Museums Scotland. For an obituary of Curle, see Graham 1956; for a biography, see Ritchie 2002.
3. Curle 1923, 99–100.
4. Curle 1923; Kaufmann-Heinimann 2013. The fish dish now finds a close parallel in the Vinkovci hoard (Croatia) – see Vulić et al. 2017. For the interpretation of the silver framework as part of a bucket, see Painter 2010a.
5. Hobbs 2016, 201–3.
6. Curle 1923, 13–19; Painter 2010b.
7. Curle 1923, nos 84–91.
8. Such as the hoards from Mildenhall (United Kingdom), Trier (Germany) and Kaiseraugst (Switzerland); Hobbs 2016; Kaufmann-Heinimann and Martin 2017; Cahn and Kaufmann-Heinimann 1984; Guggisberg and Kaufmann-Heinimann 2003.
9. Scholars often use the German term *Hacksilber*, as in German this can mean silver mistreated in a whole range of ways, not just cut up, but we will stick to the simple English hacksilver, with the same caveats; see Johns 1996a.
10. Ingemark 2014, 259–61.
11. The only other hacksilver hoard Curle discussed was one from Ballinrees in Northern Ireland (Curle 1923, 6–7).
12. Notably Grünhagen 1954 and Birley 1955.
13. Initial results are presented by various authors in Hunter and Painter 2013a.
14. The fundamental work was that of the late Kenneth Painter: Painter 2013; Hunter and Painter 2017.
15. Often into halves or quarters, which might then be further subdivided.
16. Painter 2013, 220–1.
17. The scraps of silver in the Patching hoard weigh 317.58 g, which is within 3% of a pound; the silver from Echt weighs 168.37 g of silver (half a pound to within 1.4%); see White et al. 1999; Roymans and Heeren 2015. There is some discussion over the precise weight of a Roman pound (Collingwood et al. 1991b, 1–5); we use a value of 327.45 g.
18. Hunter and Painter 2017, fig. 4.
19. At 219.85 g, they are just 0.7% over eight *unciae*.
20. Painter 2013, 224, 236, n.74; the quote is from a eulogy for the Emperor Theodosius, who defeated Magnus Maximus (for whom, see Birley 2005, 443–50).
21. Jones 1964, 623–4; Southern and Dixon 1999, 77–8; Guest 2008, 300, n.24.
22. Donatives would be paid not just on the fifth anniversary of the emperor's accession but on that of his anointed successor (Jones 1964, 623–4): in the late Empire, the emperor (Augustus) had a subordinate Caesar, while at times the Empire was split between two Augusti, each with a Caesar, all paying anniversary donatives. Contemporary illustrations referring to the official responsible for dispensing such gifts, the Count of the Sacred Largesse, show gold coins in silver vessels and other items which are probably belt buckles (Fig. 5.16). For rings and brooches, see Guggisberg 2013, 195–8; for the official, see Jones 1964, 427–38.
23. Künzl 1993; Petrovszky 2006.
24. Hunter and Painter 2017.
25. Rance (2001) discussed the evidence for Irish warriors serving in the late Roman army, for instance.
26. Guggisberg 2013, 205–7. Roymans (2017, 69) argued more generally for payment to leaders who redistributed the reward.
27. Hunter 2009b, 234–5.
28. Rau 2013a, 351–2.
29. Guest 2008, 296–7; Ploumis 2001, 63–4.
30. Guest 2008, especially 298.
31. Roymans 2017.
32. To give a taster of a wealth of material: Jørgensen and Vang

Petersen 1998 (Danish finds); Harhoiu 1977 (the Pietroasa hoard); Seipel 1999 (the Szilágysomlyó treasure); Wieczorek and Périn 2001 (broad overview of continental rich graves). The picture is complicated by the fact that some of the material of apparently Germanic character may well have been made in Roman workshops as diplomatic gifts to match local taste, such as neck-rings known from the lower Rhine or the so-called Kolben arm-rings with plain hoops and expanded terminals (Roymans 2017, 72; Quast 2013, 181–5).

33. Gold tends to dominate our view, but silver also played a role in ornament of swords and horse gear, and in personal items such as buckles and brooches, while there are rare burials in eastern Europe with intact silver vessels (e.g. from Apahida I in Romania, or Kertch in Ukraine; Wieczorek and Périn 2001, 158–60). For instance, in the sample of the 33 rich burials and hoards in the exhibition *Das Gold der Barbarenfürsten* (Wieczorek and Périn 2001), all contained gold (in two cases only gilding) but 27 also included silver, often as a minor element but sometimes dominant.

34. Bursche 1999, 2000, 2001; Guggisberg 2013, 200–2.

35. Bland and Loriot 2010, 294–310, nos 703, 706, 743. The Scottish finds come from Leochel-Cushnie and Meikle Loch of Slains (Aberdeenshire) and the banks of the River Teviot near Jedburgh (Scottish Borders). This latter coin (now in National Museums Scotland X.2001.2) is interesting for its evidence of modification. Its edges have been clipped – an unusual phenomenon in gold, though common in silver as discussed on pp 59–60. Rather than trying to garner extra gold, this was probably connected with mounting the coin as a pendant. The clipping looks irregular from the front in relation to the emperor's bust, but it makes the design on the rear, the standing figure of the emperor, look symmetrical. This may well have been interpreted as a figure of Christ – he holds a Christian *Chi-Rho* flag and a figure of Victory who could readily be interpreted as an angel. It suggests this Roman coin was reused as an early Christian item some time after it was made; the time gap involved is unknowable, though both faces of the coin show wear.

36. Bland and Loriot 2010, 334–6.

37. Between AD 364 and 455: Roymans 2017, 57.

38. Guggisberg 2013, fig. 13.8, provides a recent distribution map; for details, see Bursche 1999, 2000, 2001.

39. Some 60 single-faced medallions are known; most lack provenance, but three come from inside the Empire and eight from outside or the frontier zone (Bland 2012), suggesting they were specifically made as diplomatic gifts or payment to barbarian troops. While the larger medallions were a long-lived type, these single-faced ones are specific to the Emperor Constantine and his family in the early 4th century, suggesting they were a particular policy of this time (see Bland 2012). The Birrens medallion was of Constantine II Caesar, struck in AD 318. Two of the Irish finds were deposited at the Neolithic chambered tomb of Newgrange; the third is unprovenanced. Almost all the late Roman gold known from Ireland has come from Newgrange: a series of separate deposits have produced eight coins (two of the late 3rd century, six of the late 4th century), two early 4th-century medallions, and a selection of jewellery (Bland and Loriot 2010, 334–6; Carson and O'Kelly 1977; Janiszewski 2011). This time-hallowed site was clearly a focus of special deposits.

40. Curle 1932, 370–1; Noll 1974, 227–30; Yeroulanou 1999, 165, 234; Guggisberg 2013, 196–7. The brooch is now in the Los Angeles County Museum; a replica is in National Museums Scotland (X.FT 96).

41. Janiszewski 2012; the expanded terminals are typical of arm-rings worn in the Germanic world, but the inscription shows this one was made in the Roman world to send north as a gift, a pattern with wide parallels (Quast 2013, 181–5).

42. Hunter 2014b, 210. The medallion and brooch indicate an early 4th-century AD date for this activity – perhaps linked to preparations for and the aftermath of Constantius Chlorus' campaigns against the Picts in 305, to ensure key southern tribes kept the peace.

43. Curle 1932, 336–7, 392, fig. 36.4. The exact findspot is not recorded, though clues in various references suggest it should be traceable with a bit of endeavour in archives. The silver crossbow

Fig. 5.36: Set of replica spoons; NMS X.2015.317.1–7.

brooch from Carn Liath (discussed in chapter 4), on the northern side of the Moray Firth, suggests there were persistent links to this area.

44. The type can be paralleled in the hoard from Thetford (Norfolk) of the later 4th century; other parallels are less closely dated but consistent with such a date (Johns and Potter 1983, 93, fig. 16 no. 18; Marshall 1907, nos 816–8). Guiraud (1989, 201) noted the use of filigree was a 4th-century phenomenon.
45. See note 32.
46. Outside the hoards, silver coins are rare; only two stray finds are known, from Clatt (Aberdeenshire) and the River Clyde in Glasgow, plus one non-hoard find from Traprain (Bland, Moorhead and Walton 2013, 131–2).
47. Bland 1997, 40; Bland and Loriot 2010, 16–19.
48. Sheridan 2014.
49. Creighton 2000, 37–43 provides an interesting discussion of perceptions of metal colour.
50. Bland 1997, 40 re. British gold coinage; Hobbs 2006, 124, figs 10–14 for overall hoard patterns. The possibility of a regional 'silver economy' in late Roman Britain is suggested in Hunter and Painter 2013b, xxii.
51. Kaufmann-Heinimann 2013, 255.
52. Guest 2013.
53. Guest 2013, 96–100.
54. Abdy 2013, 107–9.
55. See divergent views in Guest 2013, Abdy 2013 and Bland, Moorhead and Walton 2013, with references to earlier work, and brief summary in Hunter and Painter 2013b, xviii–xix.
56. For similar results from other Roman silver hoards, and more background to the approaches, see Lang and Hughes 2016, with further references.
57. Lang and Hughes 2016, 245–6.
58. Lang and Holmes 1983; Lang and Hughes 2016.
59. We are grateful to George Dalgleish for helpful discussion on the topic of the replicas which has heavily informed this section. These particular cards were issued in 1937, almost twenty years after the discovery, showing the continuing impact of the Treasure.

CHAPTER SIX
Changing silver for a new world
AD 300–500

In the subdued light of the laboratory, a piece of ceramic crucible stands exposed before a beam of high-powered X-rays. As they strike the surface they cause an invisible reaction – other X-rays bounce back, characteristic of the elements on the vessel's surface. As the scientist stares at the computer screen, a tell-tale spike appears on the spectrum. This crucible had been used for melting down Roman silver.

The hillfort of Traprain Law was a powerful place in the 4th and 5th centuries AD, and its rulers controlled a wide range of craftworkers. Excavations over the last one hundred years have uncovered numerous fragments of crucibles – small heat-proof vessels used to melt metal [Fig. 6.1]. Most were used for melting bronze and brass into a

Opposite: Silver pins of the 4th and 5th centuries.

variety of ornaments and fittings, but a few show evidence for silver-working. Roman silver – perhaps bits of the Traprain Treasure, perhaps other gifts from the south – went into these melting-pots.

Iron Age crucibles were generally quite small – two of those used for silver have capacities of 7.2 cm^3 and 15.2 cm^3, representing a maximum of 75 g and 159 g of silver if filled to the brim.[1] But the objects being produced were small as well: indigenous items found at the site include a tiny decorated plaque, spiral finger-ring and fragments of pins, none weighing more than ten grams [6.2].[2] These first locally-made silver objects were fine, subtle, ornamental items, a pattern repeated elsewhere. From 4th-century deposits in a sacred cave on the Moray Firth coast at Covesea come a pair of silver tweezers (probably used for personal grooming) and a pin with a projecting, decorated head [6.3].[3]

Pins for fastening clothing were one of the main

Fig. 6.1 (above, left): Crucible used for melting silver, from Traprain Law; 50mm (height), NMS X.GVM 574.

Fig. 6.2: (above, right): Silver pins, rings and decorated mount from Traprain Law; 34mm (mount length), NMS X.GVM 120, 147, 150, 202, 269.

Fig. 6.3 (below, left): Silver tweezers and pin from Sculptor's Cave, Covesea, Moray; 42mm (length of tweezers), NMS X.HM 69 and 79.

consumers of silver – they would flash in the light, catching the eye from a distance, though the fine detail would only be visible close up. Certain types of these rare projecting ring-headed pins were regularly made of silver and widely distributed across Britain and Ireland. Archaeologists differentiate between two main types – handpins and proto-handpins [6.4a,b]. 'Handpins' get their name from the finger-like projections in a straight line across the top of the head, the curved bottom half often carrying a fine decorative design in red enamel. In 'proto-handpins' the 'fingers' are stubbier and lie on an arc.[4] The terms imply one developed from the other, which may be true, but their periods of use overlapped. A beautiful but tiny 'proto' example from Oldcroft in Gloucestershire was found with a hoard of Roman coins, proving that the type was in use by the mid-4th century AD.[5] The lower plate has red enamel to accentuate the subtle curving decoration, aesthetic

Fig. 6.4a and b: Details of the head of a proto-handpin (above) from Oldcroft, Gloucestershire; British Museum 1973,0801.1; and handpin (below), from Norrie's Law, Fife; NMS X.FC 31.

Fig. 6.5: Distribution of characteristic silver items of the 4th and 5th centuries: pins, bangles, penannular brooches and spiral finger-rings.

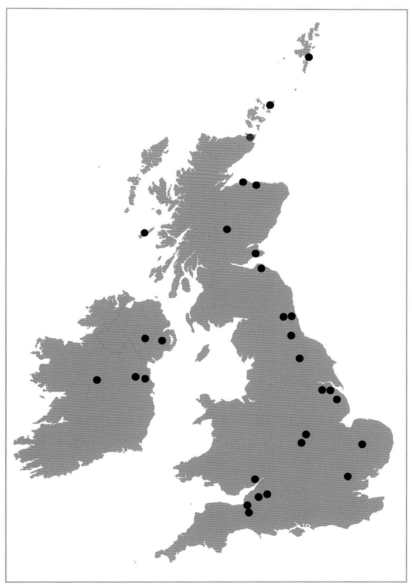

CHANGING SILVER FOR A NEW WORLD

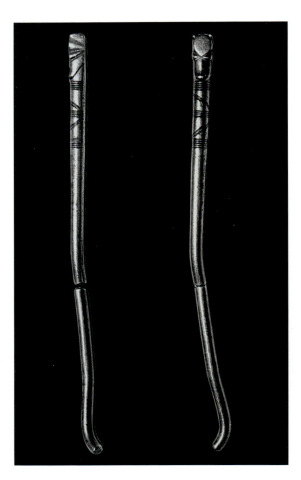

Fig. 6.6: Zoomorphic silver pin, Halton Chesters, Northumberland; 83 mm (length), Society of Antiquaries of Newcastle upon Tyne/Great North Museum 1959.5.

Fig. 6.7: Military scabbard-fitting from a hacksilver hoard at Coleraine, Northern Ireland; 69 mm (length), British Museum 1885,0815.14.

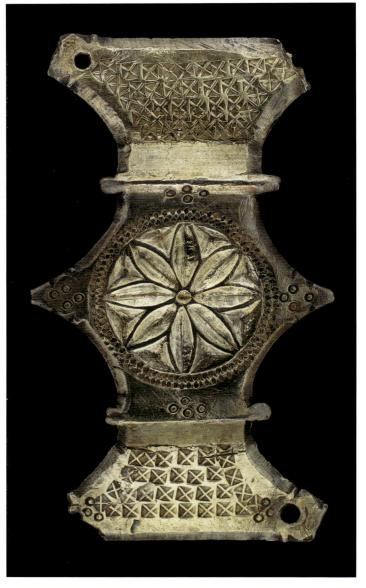

habits that proved popular over the next few centuries [6.4a]. Indeed, analysis has shown that this vibrant red enamel is actually a by-product of recycling silver, especially of purifying debased silver[6] – so the reworking of silver created the very materials for its decoration.

These pins are rare but widespread in Britain and Ireland, revealing wide-ranging links between élite groups at this time [6.5].[7] Silver versions of penannular brooches (with a pin on a C-shaped hoop which was rotated under the pin tip to hold the cloth in place) are even rarer but similarly far-flung, some with stylised animal heads as terminals [7.6]. Other forms of silver pin occur very infrequently – one has a similar animal head,[8] others bear geometric decoration derived from late Roman military

SCOTLAND'S EARLY SILVER

Fig. 6.8: Silver belt buckle with gilding and niello inlay, from a rich warrior burial at Vermand, northern France; 60 mm (height). Metropolitan Museum of Art, New York 17.192.146. © Photo SCALA, Florence 2017.

styles [6.6, 8.12].[9] On this edge of Empire, the blurring of habits across the frontier saw both silver and style move from the Roman world, especially the army, to groups around its edge. Contemporary military fashions themselves showed a strong mixture between traditional Roman habits and those of their Germanic neighbours, with styles of deeply-engraved decorative patterns (so-called 'chip-carved' ornament as it resembles wood-carving) found on belt sets and weaponry on both sides of the frontier. These were symbols of prestige in a warrior's world. For instance, a chip-carved strap end from Traprain Law [5.12] finds its best parallel in a hoard from Ejsbøl in Denmark, while gilded silver sword- and belt-fittings in a hacksilver hoard from near Coleraine in Northern Ireland [6.7] are related to examples from Germany and France, notably those from a wealthy burial from Vermand in northern France, where a warrior who had served Rome was buried with silver belt- and weapon-fittings [6.8].[10]

These chip-carved styles show links across northern Europe, but the curvilinear patterns on the handpins and proto-handpins are more typical of the islands. They are styles harking back to Iron Age traditions which persisted and developed in Roman Britain, and found renewed purpose and meaning in the changing worlds of the 4th–6th centuries AD. The pins are part of a wider set of decorative material in silver and copper alloy which used this renewed style, especially in Scotland and Ireland.[11]

Not all these silvery items are what they seem. One pin from Traprain Law looks like silver, but is actually copper alloy coated with tin to give a silvery effect, as is a brooch

CHANGING SILVER FOR A NEW WORLD

Fig. 6.9: Copper-alloy penannular brooch from Traprain Law, East Lothian, coated with tin to make it look like silver; 70mm (length), NMS X.GVM 91.

Fig. 6.10: Silver ring from Norrie's Law, Fife; 18mm (diameter), NMS X.FC 35.

from the site [6.9] and another from Castlehill near Dalry in Ayrshire [9.6].[12] This underlines the rarity of silver at the time, a metal to be desired and emulated.

Everything we have seen so far is fine and delicate – personal items which could only be appreciated from close range. But this is only part of the story. Around this time a far more impressive product dominated the visual world – massive silver chains, an example of which comes from Traprain Law itself (chapter 8; [8.15]). The ultimate source of all this material, from fine pins to massive chains, was recycled Roman silver. But how was this finite resource controlled, managed, exchanged and reworked? Two finds – a long-known hoard and a newly-discovered one – offer fresh insights. These are the subject of our next chapter.

NOTES

1. Calculations are based on the volume of a pyramid, approximating their internal plan form as a triangle and using the formula 1/3 x area x internal depth. National Museums Scotland X.GVM 574, L 40, W 43, D 25 mm; X.GVM 576, L 51, W 51, D 35 mm. In total six crucibles from the site are well-enough preserved for such estimates: the others were not used for silver-working, but for comparison they have capacities of 3.4 cm^3, 6.4 cm^3, 17.8 cm^3, and 32.9 cm^3.
2. Burley 1956, nos 120, 147, 151, 153, 202, 204, 206, 207A, 269; other silver items she noted are either Roman (nos 149–50, 157, 261), later intrusive pieces (no. 152), or were shown by analysis not to be silver (nos 148, 207 B–C).
3. Benton 1931, figs 16.1, 17.1; Stevenson 1955, fig. B10; Hunter forthcoming a. The pin is of the so-called 'corrugated' type with small beads all around the circumference.
4. Stevenson 1955, 289–92; Youngs 2005; 2016.
5. Johns 1974.
6. Rehren and Kraus 1999; Stapleton, Freestone and Bowman 1999.
7. Youngs 2005; 2016; Gavin 2013.
8. From Halton Chesters, Northumberland, the only silver one among over 40 copper-alloy examples: Smith 1960; Fowler 1963, 150, fig. 2.6; Youngs 2010, 184.
9. Gavin 2013, 428. It is noticeable that among disc-headed pins, zoomorphic pins and brooches, silver examples make up a very small proportion of the overall total, the rest being copper alloy, while the majority of proto-handpins and early handpin types are of silver (Youngs 2016). This suggests the proto-handpins and handpins were made in an area where silver was more abundant compared with the production locus of the other pins and brooches. Mould evidence points to their production in various parts of Scotland (Heald 2001; several subsequent finds confirm this Scottish distribution).
10. Curle 1923, 89–90, no. 150; Ørsnes 1988, Taf. 64 nos 4–5; Böhme 2000; Marzinzik 2013.
11. Laing 2005; 2010, 26–48; Goldberg 2015a, 160–3.
12. Burley 1956, nos 91, 118; Smith 1919, 128–9, fig 4.2.

CHAPTER SEVEN

Managing silver, managing change: Early Medieval hacksilver hoarding AD 400–600

GAULCROSS

The first discovery of silver at Gaulcross in Aberdeenshire happened with a bang, literally. In 1838, dynamite was used to blast apart two prehistoric stone circles so that the land could be cleared for cultivation. Written reports of what happened next are frustratingly vague, but it seems that quantities of silver were found, including 'pins and brooches'.[1] Most of it was then lost. Only three objects survived this 19th-century assault: a pin, a spiral bangle, and a length of intricately looped wire chain [Fig. 7.1].[2] This remnant has been a tantalising but frustrating window

Fig. 7.1 (right): The only objects that survived from the 1838 discovery of silver at Gaulcross, Aberdeenshire: a pin, a length of chain and a spiral bangle; 143 mm (pin length). Courtesy of Aberdeenshire Council Museums. Image © National Museums Scotland (IL.2001.2–4).

Opposite: A spiral-decorated mount from the hacksilver found at Norrie's Law, Fife, in 1819; NMS X.FC 29.

into what was clearly a substantial and extremely significant hoard of silver, made and buried at some point in the poorly understood transition between the late Roman Iron Age and Early Medieval periods.

Draining and digging, quarrying and building – many of our most iconic archaeological objects owe their discovery to the 19th-century eras of agricultural improvement and transport revolution. This has big implications. If you're lucky, it is possible to piece together hints about where these objects were found, why they were buried there and whether anything else was buried with them. If you are really lucky, fieldwork at the site might be able to verify some vital pieces of information, or even recover more finds.[3] This was the case at Gaulcross.

In 2013 a team from National Museums Scotland and the University of Aberdeen investigated the location of the Gaulcross stone circles [7.2]. Geophysical survey and excavation found little trace of these prehistoric monuments – their destruction had been thorough. But careful excavation and controlled metal-detecting made a startling discovery – 90 fragments of silver missed by the labourers in 1838 were located, plotted and recovered.[4] They were scattered over an area of 900 m^2, dispersed first by the destruction of the stone monuments and later dragged by ploughing. No trace of a burial pit or container was found. But though the precise archaeological context is lost, the new silver fragments have transformed our understanding of this extremely important hoard. Before 2013, the surviving objects and written sources suggested a cache of intact objects. After 2013, Gaulcross became something far more special – only the second post-Roman hacksilver hoard found in Scotland [7.3].

What does the hoard contain? It is a mixture of Roman and Early Medieval objects, almost all hacked into regular portions or packages. The Roman material includes military equipment such as belt-fittings, very small pieces

SCOTLAND'S EARLY SILVER

Fig. 7.2 (opposite): In 2013, archaeologists revisited the findspot of the Gaulcross hoard. Though there was little trace of the dynamited stone circles, excavation recovered further fragments from the hoard.

Fig. 7.3 (below): Fragments of hacksilver found at Gaulcross in 2013.

MANAGING SILVER, MANAGING CHANGE

79

of vessels, a hacked spoon handle [7.4], and *siliquae* [7.5]. These are rare finds in Scotland. This handful of coins doubled the number known, while comparable military gear and hacked plate was only known from the great Traprain Law Treasure; nothing similar is attested from settlement sites or other Scottish hoards.

Alongside the Roman silver fragments are types of objects made around and after the end of Roman Britain. There are portions of several types of Early Medieval brooch – extremely rare finds in silver. One has a tiny creature with a gaping mouth that swallows the brooch hoop [7.6]. The other is represented by two fragments – a large plain terminal and part of a twisted hoop [7.7, 7.8]. These brooches have been cut down – hacked up, ready to be recycled.

There are also parcels of folded silver [7.9], including a bundle of decorated mounts [7.10] similar to a set of bronze examples from Ireland that have been interpreted as fittings from a prestigious decorated saddle or, more plausibly, a shield.[5] Another bronze example was found at the Roman temple site at Nettleton (Wiltshire) from 4th-century deposits.[6] Many parcels are made from hacked-up bangles [7.11] and intriguingly several clasp late Roman silver coins between their folds, suggesting they were parcelled up when coinage was still available [7.12]. Other stages of the recycling process are represented too, including several ingots made from scrap silver that has been melted down but not yet turned into new objects [7.13]. There are even some missing links from the fine wire chain found in 1838 [7.15].

In one sense this hoard is itself a missing link. Archaeologists have long recognised the existence of Roman hacksilver – the impressive Traprain Law Treasure and the

Fig. 7.4 (above): Pieces of late Roman hacksilver from the Gaulcross hoard: two spoon handles, fragments from three vessels including one with a beaded rim, and two military dress fittings – a strap end and a small belt mount; 54mm (top right, length).

Fig. 7.5 (below): Eight late Roman *siliquae* from Gaulcross. These coins are rare finds from Scotland. Most have been deliberately clipped; 15mm (typical diameter).

SCOTLAND'S EARLY SILVER

80

Fig. 7.6 (above, left): Part of a small penannular brooch with terminals in the shape of stylised beast-heads. The creature swallows the hoop, and has small, bulbous eyes, a flat head and little ears; 27 mm (length).

Fig. 7.7, 7.8 (middle and below, left): Two fragments from a penannular brooch with twisted hoop and large, plain terminals. The only other examples come from the hoard of hacksilver found at Norrie's Law, Fife; 54 mm and 23 mm (length).

Fig. 7.9 (above, right): Parcel of thin silver sheet from Gaulcross; 33 mm (length).

Fig. 7.10 (below, right): Decorated mounts, possibly from a shield, which have been folded together into a parcel. The Gaulcross hoard preserves many rare or unique objects: though similar mounts are known elsewhere, these are the only silver examples to survive; 42 mm (length).

MANAGING SILVER, MANAGING CHANGE

Fig. 7.11 (above, left): Part of a silver bangle that has been cut and folded into a hacksilver parcel, from the Gaulcross hoard; 33 mm (length).

Fig. 7.12 (above, right): Part of a silver bangle with a late Roman coin clasped between its folds, from the Gaulcross hoard; 30 mm (length).

Fig. 7.13 (below, left): Ingots from the Gaulcross hoard; 113 mm (length, front ingot).

Fig. 7.14 (below, right): Enamelled decoration on the handpin found in the 19th century at Gaulcross; 19 mm (width), NMS IL.2001.1.2.

SCOTLAND'S EARLY SILVER

exciting new discovery at Dairsie (chapters 4 and 5) show the Empire managing its precious-metal supplies by turning objects into regular parcels of bullion. When that Empire ended, people in Scotland could no longer rely on the old ways of acquiring silver, so managing what they had was vital. But until very recently archaeologists had virtually no evidence of this process, leaving a gap between the last Roman silver buried in Scotland and the first complete Early Medieval silver objects to survive. No hacksilver was known after the Traprain Law hoard and only a single silver ingot had been excavated from an Early Medieval site, from the hillfort of Clatchard Craig (Fife).[7] The Gaulcross hoard provides the missing link. It shows that the practice of dividing old silver objects into regular parcels and portions outlasted Roman *Britannia*, and was taken up by the locals and used in the years after Empire. This was how the kilos of silver required to make a massive silver chain (see chapter 8) could be marshalled.

It is easy to imagine how the whole objects from Gaulcross survived their 19th-century discovery – their artistic merit and curiosity value helping to tip the scales away from Victorian recycling [7.14]. Written sources only describe the recovery of whole objects, but it seems likely that the 19th-century labourers also found hacksilver and sold it on as bullion. Our contemporary scales view this tipping point between archaeological and bullion value very differently. Though the complete objects from the Gaulcross hoard are intrinsically important, it is the hacksilver that is key to understanding the find. It also provides good evidence for dating the contents of the hoard to the 5th century, although deposition could have been later: the component of late Roman silver amongst the contents, pieces of bangles parcelled up whilst Roman coins were available, and a silver brooch type found elsewhere in bronze in the immediate post-Roman period. As we have seen already (page 26), shifts in society in north-east Scotland from around the 3rd century AD led to centuries of near-invisible archaeology, thanks to disruption bound up with Roman manipulation of local power politics and the destabilising arrival of silver. The Gaulcross hoard falls towards the end of this period of particularly problematic archaeology and gives us a snapshot of material that otherwise simply does not survive, preserving types almost entirely lost to the Early Medieval silversmith's crucible.

Fig. 7.15 (above, left and right): The length of silver chain found at Gaulcross in the 19th century (left), with a further wire link (right) recovered in 2013; 32mm (length).

Fig. 7.16 (overleaf): The surviving portion of the hacksilver hoard found at Norrie's Law, Fife, in 1819. Like Gaulcross, most of the silver was lost soon after its discovery.

MANAGING SILVER, MANAGING CHANGE

NORRIE'S LAW

The Gaulcross hoard is not unique. One other post-Roman hacksilver hoard is known from Scotland, also unearthed during the 19th century. Like Gaulcross it was labourers who found silver at a small hillock, known locally as Norrie's Law, near Largo in Fife during 1819. This discovery was twice kept secret. First, the workers failed to alert their employer and landowner, General Durham. By the time he did find out, most of the silver had been bought by silversmiths as bullion. Though he recovered what he could, General Durham then chose not to make the discovery public, instead keeping the salvaged silver quietly at his house for the next twenty years. Only when a local Fife antiquary called George Buist visited General Durham's estate in 1839 did the silver come to public attention. Buist recognised the importance of the surviving fragments and set about finding out more – about how the silver was found and what had been lost. His report, published twenty years after the discovery, is the main source of information about this spectacular find.[8]

All told, 170 fragments of silver from the Norrie's Law hoard remain today [7.16], though this is only a fraction – around 750 g of the estimated 12.5 kg of silver that had been found.[9] Most of the surviving silver has been neglected over the years, overlooked in favour of a handful of star objects: a pair of leaf-shaped plaques and pair of handpins. Three of these four pieces feature Pictish symbols, a kind of script unique to Scotland which is found mainly on sculptured stone monuments in the north and east of the country.[10] Though the dating and meaning of symbols has long been debated and remains contentious today, one thing is clear – symbols on portable objects are extremely unusual. Only two other examples on metal survive, on the terminals of two silver chains (page 101).[11] But all is not what it seems in the Norrie's Law hoard. Two of the three objects with Pictish symbols are 19th-century copies.

SCOTLAND'S EARLY SILVER

84

Fig. 7.17 (right, above): The pairs of handpins and Pictish symbol-decorated mounts attributed to the Norrie's Law hoard; 170mm (pin length), NMS X.FC 30–31, 33–34.

Fig. 7.18 and 7.19 (middle): Traces of enamel are preserved in the channels of decoration on the genuine symbol-decorated mount, visible under magnification in a scanning electron microscope.

Fig. 7.20 (below): Tips of the two Pictish symbol-decorated mounts. Damage on the genuine mount (left) is replicated on the 19th-century copy (right); NMS X.FC 33–34.

FORGERIES OR FACSIMILES?

The silver salvaged from Norrie's Law and donated to Scotland's national archaeological collection in the 19th century contained two sets of objects – matching handpins and leaf-shaped plaques [7.17]. Pairs of virtually identical objects are exceedingly rare: no other examples survive from Early Medieval Scotland. Added to this, both of the plaques and one of the handpins bear Pictish symbols, further marking them out as special and significant objects. But all was not what it seemed.

The Glenmorangie Research Project began to examine the objects more closely to establish just how similar the pairs really were. The plaques differ in small decorative details (one has a hard border, the other just a hint of one), and scientific analysis identified more differences. The symbols on both plaques were filled with a red substance, but though we expected this to be enamel it turned out to be an organic substance – probably wax that had been added in the 19th century. Only one of the plaques had in fact ever been enamelled – tiny traces were found surviving in nooks and crannies of the engraved symbol [7.18, 7.19].

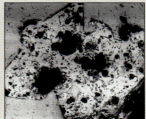

Analysis revealed more differences. The two plaques had been made differently (one was cast, while the other had been worked with a hammer) and from different recipes of silver alloy. But while different to each other, one of the plaques was made from a similar recipe to one of handpins, and both were very different from the rest of the hoard.

Looking again at the 19th-century report of the hoard's discovery provided a clue. It showed that only one plaque and pin, not two, had been recovered by General Durham in 1819. The other plaque and pin were found in 1839, twenty years later. The report's writer, George Buist, believed them to be part of

MANAGING SILVER, MANAGING CHANGE

Fig. 7.21 (left): Pewter facsimiles of items from the Norrie's Law hoard, made in 1839 by Robert Robertson, the same silversmith who had bought portions of the hoard for bullion twenty years earlier. Fife Cultural Trust Collection. Image © National Museums Scotland.

Fig. 7.22 and 7.23 (below): Symbol-decorated plaques and handpins: genuine (left), 1839 pewter facsimile (middle) and 1839 silver copy (right). Fife Cultural Trust Collection. Images © National Museums Scotland.

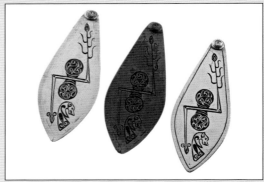

the lost hoard that had been sold to silversmiths and then rescued thanks to his enquiries. But it seems he was misled. The 1839 plaque and pin are made from a silver alloy too lacking in impurities to be ancient. They are 19th-century copies.[12]

They are so similar to the genuine plaque and pin that they must be direct copies – damage on the genuine plaque is replicated on the other, showing an impression was made and a mould created from it [7.20]. So who made the copies and how did they get mixed up with the genuine silver? One of the silversmiths who had (illegally) bought part of the hoard in 1819 was also one of the main sources of information about what had been found and lost. It is understandable that the antiquarian George Buist sought this jeweller out and quizzed him on the discovery. The same silversmith was also commissioned by Buist to make pewter copies of the hoard's star objects [7.21] – in the days before photography was commonplace, accurate copies were an important tool for publicity and research. Buist wanted to use these pewter facsimiles to help gather information and recover lost silver objects. Indeed, he thought he had succeeded when he reported the recovery of the second pin and plaque.[13] Instead, it seems that the silversmith used the moulds from his (legitimate) pewter commission to make several (illegitimate) silver copies [7.22, 7.23]. Buist clearly thought them to be genuine, but this was not the case.

Fig. 7.24 (left): This finger-ring is one of only a handful of complete objects in the Norrie's Law hoard. It is clearly worn; ribbing around part of its length has been smoothed away; 17.5 mm (diameter), NMS X.FC 35.

Fig. 7.25 (below): One of two almost identical brooches from the Norrie's Law hoard, both lacking their pins. This brooch type was unparalleled until identical fragments were recovered in 2013 from Gaulcross; 147 mm (diameter), NMS X.FC 36.

Beyond the single genuine symbol-decorated plaque and handpin, what else survives from the Norrie's Law hoard? There are very few intact objects – a worn spiral finger-ring decorated with ribbing [7.24] and a substantial brooch hoop, missing its pin [7.25] (matched by another broken example with a modern repair). The handpin is also complete, though it was repaired in antiquity – usually cast in a single piece, solder on the back of the head suggests this pin had broken in two. But aside from these whole objects, the rest is hacksilver – items in the process of being cut and hacked into portions. The beautiful spiral-decorated plaque with its uneven edges is an example of hacking in action [7.26]. The many pieces of thin silver sheet are also hacksilver, once parts of parcels like those found in the Gaulcross hoard [7.27]. But unlike the Gaulcross silver, these parcels have been unfolded, most likely by General Durham or his labourers soon after the discovery. Unfolding caused the thin pieces of silver to snap, meaning that each is now in several pieces, though careful jigsaw work has put some back together. Many have a tiny punch mark at the top and bottom, a tap with a hammer and point to help keep these springy bundles of silver from opening unintentionally.

Identifying the original objects is another jigsaw puzzle. Pieces of silver sheet seem to belong to at least one delicate vessel with an embossed rim [7.28]. There are mounts decorated with motifs also found on bindings in the Gaulcross hoard [7.29]. As well as the complete ring and brooch, there are fragments of other prestigious dress objects – pieces from another ring, part of a miniature handpin, and many portions of bangle that had once been folded in parcels like the Gaulcross hoard [7.30]. These fragmentary personal objects – pins, brooches, bangles and rings – sit well with the products of early silver-working at Traprain Law [6.3]. But both hoards also contain unusual or enigmatic objects. This rarity is a real hindrance, though parallels from far beyond Scotland can prove insightful.

MANAGING SILVER, MANAGING CHANGE

Fig. 7.26 (above, left): A mount decorated with finely executed, high-relief spirals, from Norrie's Law. The object was in the process of being cut down, and its original function remains unknown; 127mm (height), NMS X.FC 29.

Fig. 7.27 (above, middle): A silver jigsaw puzzle – a parcel of silver sheet from Norrie's Law that had broken when unfolded in the 19th century and has only recently been reassembled; 180mm (length).

Fig. 7.28 (below, left): Amongst the Norrie's Law hoard are pieces of a vessel with a thin beaded rim. Some have clearly been cut and folded into hacksilver parcels.

Fig. 7.29 (above, right): Mounts from Norrie's Law decorated with designs also found in the Gaulcross hoard; 18mm (width).

Fig. 7.30 (below, right): Many objects in the Norrie's Law hoard are very rare. These bangles are virtually unknown, except from within the Gaulcross hoard; 18mm (width).

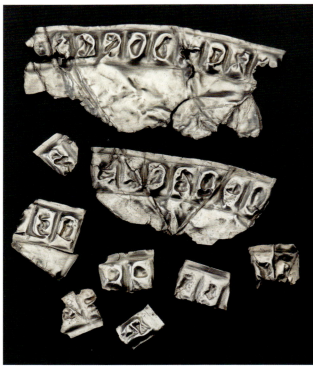
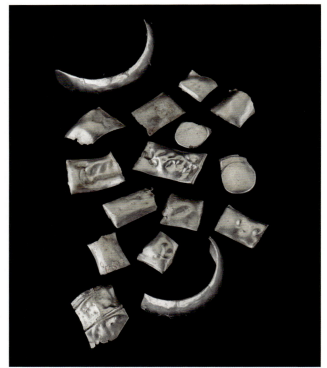

SCOTLAND'S EARLY SILVER

Fig. 7.31: Symbol-decorated plaque, Norrie's Law; 91mm (length), NMS X.FC 34.

Fig. 7.32: Composite helmet from Morken, Nordrhein-Westfalen, Germany, with decorated gilt copper-alloy sheets over iron; © Jürgen Vogel, LVR Landesmuseum, Bonn, 55,435.

PURSUING A PICTISH HELMET

One of the most puzzling items from the Norrie's Law hoard is a teardrop-shaped plaque, 91mm long, engraved with Pictish symbols – a beast's head, and two decorated discs which are joined together and crossed by a Z-shaped rod with ornate ends [7.31].[14] A faint groove bounds a margin which is less well-polished than the rest. The top has a curious raised decorated boss, hollow on the underside.

Its function has long been a mystery. Ideas have varied from a piece of scale armour to a votive plaque or some 'mystic or magical purpose'[15] – though most scholars have tended to shrug their shoulders and focus solely on the decoration. But by casting our net beyond Britain, we think we have a plausible answer. Plaques of exactly this form are found on Early Medieval helmets on the continent, especially in France and Germany. They consist of an iron framework with teardrop-shaped insets, often decorated, filling the gaps [7.32].[16] The continental examples were typically riveted to the framework, but there are examples of plaques clamped in channels. The Norrie's Law plaque has the required shape, while its worn edges suggest that it has been squeezed in a frame. Could it come from such a helmet?[17]

Questions remain. It is smaller than other surviving helmet plaques, and the curious boss at one end remains a puzzle (although it could be a decorative cap for an underlying structural rivet). It is also flat, which would make it difficult to fit into the curving form of a helmet. But the flattening may be recent, while other anomalies can be explained away by the material. This is the only silver example known – others are made from copper alloy or iron, sometimes coated in silver or gold – and it is little surprise that precious metal was used more sparingly. But we should not be misled into seeking exact analogy with the continental finds. Rather than a derivative Pictish copy of such a composite helmet, this was an inspiration or version of one, taking the idea and modifying it. We think the similarities in form are more than coincidence: is this our first surviving part of a Pictish helmet?

MANAGING SILVER, MANAGING CHANGE

CONNECTED HOARDS

The hoards from Norrie's Law and Gaulcross are connected in several ways. The hacksilver parcels and the combination of Roman and local silver objects are unknown from anywhere elsewhere in Scotland, though there must have been more such hoards, and more may yet appear. Specific objects also bind the two hoards together. The handpins have long linked the finds in scholars' minds, and the 2013 discovery at Gaulcross adds further parallels, in the bangles and in a brooch type not found beyond these two Scottish hoards. But there are differences too, though whether they are simply a product of chance – what survived the 19th century – or archaeologically meaningful is frustratingly unclear. For instance, no ingots survive amongst the Norrie's Law silver, though they would be a natural candidate for Georgian recycling. And some object types are only found in one of the hoards: silver sheet from the Norrie's Law hoard with a bossed rim, or the animal-headed brooch in the Gaulcross hoard, for example. But overall the impression is of two very closely linked hoards, found around 130 miles apart.

What should we make of this similarity? Though the hoards used to be thought of as dating to the 7th or even 8th century,[18] new research and the 2013 discoveries place them closer to the 5th century.[19] Our understanding of the political geography of Scotland in the 5th and 6th centuries is limited, it is fair to say. Roman sources recorded some tribal names between the 1st and 4th centuries, labels which have been pasted across Scotland by archaeologists and historians with varying degrees of confidence. Later sources, all written outside of Scotland, preserved names of Early Medieval peoples, kingdoms and regions. But how far these Early Medieval entities can be projected back in time, and where the Iron Age tribes and Early Medieval peoples connect (or not), has involved some educated guesswork. The Early Medieval Scottish mainland north of the Forth is often called 'Pictland', but this label is misleading. We have no historical evidence for whether Pictland was a single, coherent political entity during the 5th and 6th centuries. This makes the two silver hoards even more important as valuable sources of evidence during this shadowy period. A common sense of cultural identity embracing the regions in which these two hoards were found may not have developed until the later 7th century.[20] But even then, this Pictland consisted of multiple kingdoms, distinct political units that were vying for supremacy. Apparent cultural connections masked significant political divisions.

What then to make of the two hoards' similarities? We must remember how patchy our evidence is – such finds are just the surviving tip of a much larger, mostly lost, iceberg of silver objects used across the north. Given how much has been lost, we should be cautious of over-interpretation. But the links are telling: the hoards show a common access to raw material and shared mindset regarding its management. What was the purpose of marshalling quantities of silver? As explored in chapter 6, silver had been gathered and recycled in Scotland since the 3rd or 4th century AD, used to make local types of personal objects such as pins and other small items of decorated metalwork. This clearly required a source of silver, though many of the earliest datable types are small objects requiring only modest amounts of the precious metal. The Norrie's Law and Gaulcross hoards include a handful of objects made

Fig. 7.33: Two silver spiral finger-rings buried as Roman Iron Age votive offerings at the prehistoric site of Newgrange, Co. Meath. They are very similar to examples from the Norrie's Law hoard, which was also buried at the site of a much older monument. © Reproduced with the kind permission of the National Museum of Ireland.

Fig. 7.34: Hacksilver hoard from Mannerup, Denmark. Danish hacksilver hoards span the Roman and Early Medieval periods, and like Norrie's Law and Gaulcross most contain a mixture of Roman and local types of objects. Unlike the Scottish examples, the Danish hoards contain both silver and gold, a product of different precious metals inheritances from the Roman world. © Museum Organisation ROMU.

from more substantial amounts of silver, particularly the brooches made from solid silver bars twisted into a hoop with thick flattened terminals [see 7.25]. This period probably also saw the manufacture of massive silver chains (chapter 8), the most intensive users of silver that Scotland had yet produced, each of which required 1–3 kilos of bullion. At a time of limited new supplies, careful management of silver resources was needed.

So are the Norrie's Law and Gaulcross hoards a product of efficient resource management? Perhaps, but while there are sound material reasons for gathering scrap and broken objects together, other motivations are possible. The creation of Roman hacksilver often correlated with periods of economic uncertainty, while hoarding is perhaps more likely during periods of crisis and strife. Was the burial of Norrie's Law and Gaulcross symptomatic of economic or political instability? If so, they may represent payments or bribes made in true Roman fashion, gifted to make friends and influence people.

However, the manner of their burial hints at something more than a purely economic motivation. Both were deposited at much older monuments – a prehistoric stone circle and a likely Bronze Age burial mound. This is part of a pattern of Early Medieval meddling in and appropriation of prehistoric monuments and landscapes across northwestern Europe.[21] Such reuse has been linked to the development of an increasingly hierarchical society and the emergence of high-status rulers seeking new ways to show their authority and legitimise their power by making connections with the past.[22] Stories, traditions and myths, all lost to us now, will also have been important in deciding where to build and bury, influencing which old places were reimagined as potent and powerful Early Medieval centres. In Ireland, the Neolithic passage grave at Newgrange, Co.

MANAGING SILVER, MANAGING CHANGE

Meath, became a focus for Roman Iron Age religious activity and, later still, an inauguration site for Early Medieval kings.[23] Tellingly perhaps, Roman silver and gold was also buried at Newgrange, as were two silver finger-rings [7.33] very similar to those from the Norrie's Law hoard. This striking parallel, both in material and burial context, suggests the precious deposits at Newgrange and Norrie's Law may belong to contemporary practices and beliefs. However, at Newgrange the silver and gold objects were buried individually or in small caches rather than as a substantial hoard. What about Norrie's Law and Gaulcross? Controlled modern excavation can distinguish between a single, large hoard, and the repeated burial of individual objects at the same site. Here we feel the loss of archaeological context keenly – this is just the information lacking for Norrie's Law and Gaulcross, though the objects themselves provide some clues. The Scottish hoards contain multiple examples of certain object types – for instance, the bangles or pieces from a dish with a beaded rim [7.28, 7.30] – and multiple parcels made from a single object [7.16]. This profile is more in keeping with substantial hoards than with repeated small deposits.

Just as Roman hacksilver found in Scotland is part of a bigger story (chapter 5), so too is this silver that came next. Hoards of hacked and broken precious-metal objects from the 4th–6th centuries have been found elsewhere in north-western Europe. Denmark in particular provides a good comparison, with around twenty hoards of fragmented Roman and Early Medieval objects known [7.34].[24] But unlike Scotland, the Danish hoards often contain both silver and gold – Scotland again stands out as unusual in its use of silver alone. Also unlike Scotland, many of the Danish hoards were buried in or near settlements – by fence-posts or in doorways.[25] They have sometimes been interpreted as jewellers' caches, but are more plausibly seen as belonging to individual families, representing their economic, social and political capital. These Danish hoards show that similar processes of resource management, the gathering and recycling of precious metals, were necessary elsewhere along and beyond the former Roman frontier. There, as in Scotland, people who had been raised on Roman metals needed to go it alone. And there, as in Scotland, the people and the practices that filled vacuums left by the Roman Empire shaped the development of Early Medieval kingdoms.[26]

Whether the end of the Roman Empire heralded calamitous change or continuity (and scholars have hotly debated this issue),[27] it seems that a careful balance of old and new was required by Early Medieval élites. In Scotland, silver provided continuity – literally, in the recycling that was required to gather it, and symbolically in the connotations it carried of past relations with Rome. But new power symbols were required. Enter the massive silver chains.

NOTES

1. Stuart 1867, 75, pl. 9; Coles 1906, 188.
2. Stevenson and Emery 1964.
3. Reinvestigating the 19th-century discovery of iconic objects in the national collection is the subject of an Art Fund New Collecting award, held by Martin Goldberg at National Museums Scotland.
4. Noble et al. 2016.
5. Mounts from Hillquarter, Co. Westmeath, Ireland: Kelly 2001.
6. Wedlake 1982, 207, fig. 86, no. 13.
7. Close-Brooks 1986.
8. Buist 1839; the history of the find is reviewed in Graham-Campbell 1991.
9. Buist 1839, though this estimate may be inflated and should be treated with some caution: Graham-Campbell 1991; Youngs 2013, 414.
10. Fraser 2008.
11. A further metal symbol-bearing plaque, now lost, was found in the late 18th century in the parish of Monifieth. It appears to have been discovered when a large mound, perhaps an earlier burial cairn, was disturbed by the creation of a new drain: Roger 1880; Fraser 2008, 138.
12. See Goldberg and Blackwell 2013.
13. Buist 1839, preface.
14. The second similar plaque from the hoard has been shown to be a 19th-century copy – see pages 85–6.
15. Usefully reviewed by Graham-Campbell 1991, 250–1; the quote is from Way 1849, 255.
16. Vogt 2006.
17. As we were pursuing this interpretation, we realised that the former Keeper of the National Museum of Antiquities of Scotland, Robert Stevenson, had anticipated our thoughts 25 years ago in a passing remark in one of his final papers; Stevenson 1993, 20.
18. Summarised by Graham-Campbell 1991; based on Stevenson 1955; Stevenson and Emery 1964; Henderson 1967.
19. See Blackwell and Goldberg forthcoming.
20. Fraser 2009, 44–54, 114, 136–8, 224–8, 253, 373–9.
21. Forteviot in Perthshire is documented as the location of a 9th-century palace royal palace. Excavation there since 2007 has revealed the most extensive evidence for Early Medieval interventions in a prehistoric landscape yet found in Scotland (Campbell et al. forthcoming).
22. See, for example, Bradley 1987; Driscoll 1998; Semple 2013; Schot, Newman and Bhreathnach 2011.
23. Carson and O'Kelly 1977.
24. Dyhrfjeld-Johnsen 2013.
25. Rau 2013b, 191–2.
26. This topic is the subject of a project funded by the Arts & Humanities Research Council and led by National Museums Scotland in collaboration with Andreas Rau from the Centre for Baltic and Scandinavian Archaeology, at the Stiftung Schleswig-Holsteinische Landesmuseen Schloss Gottorf. 'Silver, status and society: the transition between late Roman and Early Medieval Europe' has created a network of scholars working on comparable material across Europe. It aims to better contextualise and compare the use of silver and its role in the development of Early Medieval Europe.
27. For example, see Gerrard 2013; Goldsworthy 2009; Heather 2007; Pohl 1997; Ward-Perkins 2005.

CHAPTER EIGHT
New power symbols: massive silver chains
AD 300–500

Handling the massive silver chains is an enormous privilege. The reality of the sheer amount of silver is striking: the links make a special kind of heavy clink as they shift, and holding a chain up for any length of time is hard work. But they have not always been appreciated or recognised: one found in the 18th century was broken up in an attempt to identify the metal, perhaps because it was beyond the realms of reason that something so large could be made from silver.[1]

We have given these objects the name 'massive silver chains' because they represent the most conspicuous consumption of an extremely precious resource [Fig. 8.1]. Nothing else from this time uses anything like the same amount of silver. Even the most elaborate Early Medieval brooch ever found in Scotland contains only an eighth of the silver used to make the largest chain. Handling a massive silver chain brings two questions to the fore. Why wear a three-kilo chain around your neck? And when that chain is made from solid silver, why bury it in the ground?

THE SURVIVING CHAINS

The massive silver chains are a power symbol unique to Scotland. But of course Scotland did not exist at this time. Instead, the distribution of the massive chains tells us that certain areas to the north of the Roman frontier zone were rich in recycled Roman silver and prized it above other metals. The chains cluster in south-eastern Scotland, from South Lanarkshire in the west to the Borders and Lothians in the east. A smaller group is scattered along the north-east coast, from Aberdeenshire to Inverness [8.2]. In total, parts of nine survive today (none are now entirely complete) [8.3], while two further chains were found and lost

Opposite: Massive silver chain from Borland, South Lanarkshire; NMS X.FC 264.

Fig. 8.1: The massive silver chains. The nine surviving examples (all now incomplete) together weigh over 11.5 kg.

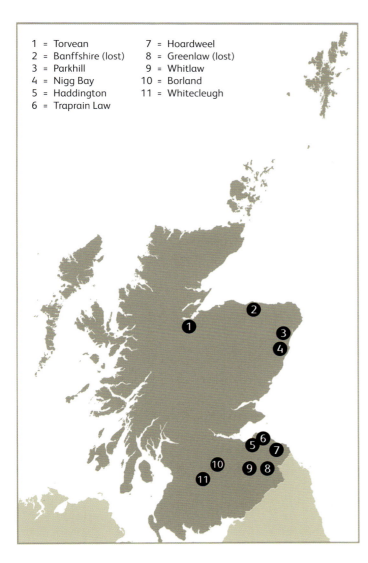

1 = Torvean
2 = Banffshire (lost)
3 = Parkhill
4 = Nigg Bay
5 = Haddington
6 = Traprain Law
7 = Hoardweel
8 = Greenlaw (lost)
9 = Whitlaw
10 = Borland
11 = Whitecleugh

Fig. 8.2 (left): Findspots of the silver chains.

Fig. 8.3 (below): The nine surviving silver chains. From the top: Hoardweel, Torvean, Haddington, Traprain Law, Borland, Whitecleugh, Parkhill, Whitlaw, Nigg (far left); 442 mm (length of top chain).

in the 19th century.[2] All eleven discoveries were made by chance, during quarrying, canal construction or agricultural improvements. This severely limits what we can know about them – none has come from controlled modern excavations and all lack even basic information about their burial context.

The body of a massive chain is made up of pairs of solid silver links, with slightly larger rings at either end: a pair at one end and a single at the other [8.4]. These three larger end-rings were held by a broad, horseshoe-shaped clasp; to fasten or unfasten the chain, the single end-ring would be slipped out through the clasp's gap. We assume that the clasp would be worn at the front with the gap showing because two of the five surviving examples are decorated here [8.5, 8.7]. Though they look very similar, there are subtle differences amongst the surviving chains. Apart from the presence or absence of decoration, the most apparent difference is in the size of the links. The body of the Torvean (Inverness) chain is made from the largest individual rings – 33 in total, with an average weight of almost 90 grams per link[3] – while the Haddington (East Lothian) chain has by far the smallest. It uses almost double the number of links, each around 10 g [8.6].[4] The clasps also differ in size, while two – Parkhill, Aberdeenshire, and Borland, South Lanarkshire – were either made differently or adapted at a later date. While the rest are solid D-shaped

NEW POWER SYMBOLS

97

Fig. 8.4 (above, left): This chain was found whilst digging the Caledonian Canal at Torvean, near Inverness; NMS X.FC 148.

Fig. 8.5 (above, right): The chain from Parkhill, Aberdeenshire, one of two examples that bear Pictish symbols on the clasp; NMS X.FC 147.

Fig. 8.6 (below): The largest chain, Torvean (top) and the smallest, from Haddington, East Lothian (bottom); 455mm (top chain), NMS X.FC 148, 149.

Fig. 8.7 (opposite): The five surviving clasps. Two (Parkhill and Borland) show an economising feature – metal has been saved from inside the clasp where it would not be readily visible when worn. Top to bottom, left to right: Hoardweel, Whitecleugh, Whitlaw, Parkhill, Borland.

SCOTLAND'S EARLY SILVER

98

Fig. 8.8: The chain from Hoardweel, Scottish Borders, is made from what appears to be undiluted Roman silver; NMS IL.2009.15.5.

clasps, these two have an I-shaped profile, a way of saving silver from the inside of the ring where it would not have been easily visible [8.7].

WHO WORE THE CHAINS?

Each chain represents a massive investment by people capable of marshalling several kilograms of silver. This tells us something of the power of those who controlled their manufacture and use. The length of the two near-complete chains provides the only indication of who would have worn them. The chain from Torvean has all three end-rings intact (so we know its length is complete), but the clasp is now missing, though it was present when the chain was found in 1808. The chain from Hoardweel (Scottish Borders) has its clasp and two end-rings intact but the third is broken, meaning it is possible that some of the paired links have been lost [8.8]. Still, these examples give us the best idea of the size of a complete chain, and both would fit only a fairly small neck diameter, that of a woman or an adolescent.[5]

While other chains may have been longer (although none are, in their current state), at least these two appear not to have been designed for men. There are good reasons to keep the chains as short as possible: not only to limit the amount of silver required, but also to manage their weight. If any longer than necessary, their substantial mass would be borne, painfully, by the neck, dragging it down; any individual wearing the mass of the Torvean chain would carry the weight on their shoulders, bearably if not comfortably. Such a snug fit might require adaptation over the years – the addition or removal of links to suit new wearers – though analysis of the silver alloys does not so far provide convincing indications of this.[6] Certainly, the consistency of the shape and size of the links argues strongly against their use as any kind of portable bank, a source of silver from which links could be casually taken off and used as currency. These chains were designed to be worn.

NEW POWER SYMBOLS

At the time they were made the chains were the heaviest personal ornament ever seen in Scotland. Their scale – head and shoulders above any other precious-metal object – means they should be seen as a kind of regalia rather than jewellery. Indeed, the largest chain is almost twice as heavy as the Crown of Scotland, altered into its current form for James V in 1540.[7] Made around a thousand years later than the chains, the Crown of Scotland is solid gold, ornamented with garnets, amethysts, freshwater pearls and enamel, and elaborated with powerful symbols including a Christian cross, a globe and *fleurs-de-lis*. In contrast, most of the massive silver chains are entirely undecorated – their visual impact came from their material, size and form. The two that are decorated bear their own powerful but enigmatic motifs, rendered in red enamel – Pictish symbols [8.9].

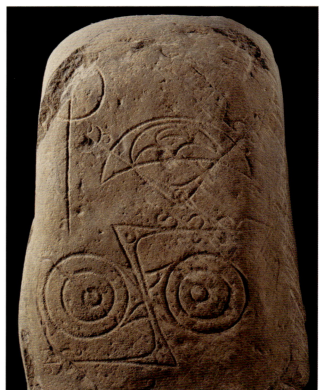

Fig. 8.9: Two of the chain clasps are decorated with Pictish symbols – Whitecleugh (South Lanarkshire, left) and Parkhill (Aberdeenshire).

Fig. 8.10 (right): Pictish symbols on a stone from Invereen, Inverness-shire; NMS X.IB 227.

Fig. **8.11**: The chain from Whitecleugh, with its decorated clasp; NMS X.FC 150.

POWERFUL SYMBOLS

Pictish symbols are a script found carved onto free-standing stone monuments in eastern Scotland north of the Forth [8.10], but very rarely on portable objects. Though they have been the subject of research and fascination for centuries, fundamental questions about their date, purpose and development remain.[8] In the past they were often equated with Pictland, thought to define the extent of a coherent cultural, political or ethnic group. Indeed, these massive chains used to be known as 'Pictish silver chains', though only two of the surviving nine are decorated with symbols and the majority (including one bearing symbols) were found in southern Scotland, well beyond Pictland's likely border.[9] But of course chains are portable objects that could pass between hands, and the symbol-bearing clasps are detachable from the body of the chains. Because of this, they cannot tell us reliably about where the Pictish symbols were developed.

Though the two symbol-bearing chains tend to be considered along with the sculptured stones, in fact a number of characteristics of the designs set them apart. Both chain clasps include unusual elements not found on sculpture: a pair of triangles and two sets of triple dots on the Parkhill example [8.9]; a zig-zag border on the Whitecleugh chain [8.11]. The Whitecleugh terminal also carries a symbol very common on the stones (a pair of discs separated by a bent arrow-like rod), but here it is rendered differently, in mirror image compared with almost every stone example. And while stone monuments mostly always feature pairs of symbols, the chain from Parkhill does not. The chains do not follow the same conventions that governed symbols carved on stones. Pictish symbols are also found carved into a few cave walls, as at East Wemyss in Fife; and here, as on the chains, there is more fluidity in the orientation and composition than on the free-standing stone monuments. It seems that on chains (and in caves) symbol-usage was not as regimented as the bulk of the carved stones. Could this imply that they were carved for a different purpose, or were they made at a different time from the more standard stone monuments?

DATING THE CHAINS

Dating the chains is a real problem. In the absence of good evidence, archaeologists have dated them broadly to between the 5th and 7th centuries AD. They are a remarkably coherent group, with surprisingly little variation in design or manufacture, which might suggest they were

Fig. 8.12: A disc-headed pin probably from Ireland, decorated in a local version of late Roman military-style metalwork. The combination of enamel and silver, and details of the decoration, link the decorated chain clasps to these prestigious hybrid silver pins; 20 mm (head diameter), British Museum, 1888,0719.100.

made over quite a short period of time. But of course traditions can be pervasive, particularly when it comes to powerful objects or symbols, so this similarity may not be a good guide to their date.

In the wider context of silver use in Scotland it certainly makes sense to see them as belonging to the time when peak supplies would have been available, during or soon after the collapse of Roman power and economy in the west. Until recently, the Traprain Law hoard was the only guide to the availability of hacksilver bullion in Scotland, and its deposition in the early 5th century provided a reasonable starting-point for dating the chains. However, the newly discovered Dairsie hoard (chapter 4) now shows that Roman bullion was present in Scotland from the later 3rd century AD – in theory, this means that the chains could have been developed over a hundred years earlier than previously thought. Preliminary scientific analysis indicated that the body of the Hoardweel chain was made from a silver alloy very similar to late Roman plate, suggesting manufacture either contemporary with or soon after the arrival of hacksilver payments from the Roman Empire.[10] Other chains are made from more variable alloys, but many factors beyond just the passing of time could explain this variation, from choices made by the silversmith to treatments inflicted on the chains after they were found. More scientific analysis of the silver alloys may help to unravel this problem in the future.

Other clues support an early date for the chains. The combination of silver with red enamel inlay and details of the motifs link the two decorated chains to 4th/5th-century pins found in small numbers across Britain and Ireland.[11] The decoration on these pins, which include handpins [6.4] and elaborately decorated disc-headed pins [8.12], has been interpreted as a British and Irish reaction to late Roman military metalwork.[12] The similarities in material and elements of the designs suggest that the chains (and indeed the Pictish symbols themselves), grew out of the same processes of interaction and hybridisation of local and Roman material culture. The symbol-decorated plaque from Norrie's Law can also be interpreted as a product of this fusion – a component from a type of helmet that other 'barbarian' tribes developed along and beyond the continental Roman frontiers (page 89).

Why a neck-chain? Lengths of much smaller bronze double-linked chains are known from Iron Age Scotland, and though their function is unknown it is possible that they are cousins to their massive silver counterparts. Examples have been excavated from Iron Age sites, mostly in northern Scotland – Moray, Orkney, Shetland and Skye [8.13].[13] An example from Leckie in Stirlingshire was found strung between two enamelled Roman brooches.[14] A more substantial length of bronze double-link chain is known from 4th-century destruction deposits at the civil settlement attached to the Roman fortress at Caerleon, Gwent.[15] An unusual kind of Roman silver necklace made up of three lengths of double-link chain, worn choker-style around the neck, was buried with a jewellery hoard at the frontier fort of Great Chesters (Northumberland).[16] But

SCOTLAND'S EARLY SILVER

Fig. 8.13: Length of copper-alloy chain, made from pairs of small links, from High Pasture Cave on Skye. Iron Age chains like these may be ancestors of the massive silver examples, although they are substantially smaller in size; 7.5 mm (link diameter).

Fig. 8.14: Iron Age gold torcs found at Blair Drummond, Stirling. Torcs continued to be used in the Roman period and probably inspired the design of the massive silver neck ornaments; 147 mm (diameter of right torc), NMS X.2011.6.1–4.

the massive silver chains are significantly larger than any of these Roman or Iron Age examples. Though they may be related, the massive chains signal a significant change – in the choice of silver rather than bronze, and in the ability and desirability of wielding and wearing substantial amounts of the precious metal.

The form of the massive chains echoes an earlier power symbol – the Iron Age torc. Torcs were also worn around the neck, often with a gap at the front, though most styles used a more rigid design than the chains. They were a power symbol found across Iron Age Europe and beyond, a widespread idea that was made in different materials and styles in different areas.[17] Many examples, like the torcs made between 300–100 BC and buried at Blair Drummond, Stirling [8.14], were golden, though in areas with exploited silver sources (including Spain, Portugal and eastern Europe) silver torcs were more common. These Iron Age torcs pre-date the chains by several hundred years. But torc use continued in the Roman period. In Roman Britain, new forms of bronze torc developed,[18] while the Roman army awarded torcs as a military decoration [9.4], and they continued in use as a military status symbol in the 3rd and 4th centuries AD.[19] The shape of the torc was evoked in the various styles of penannular brooch popular in Britain's northern military zone, which continued to be used and developed in the centuries after the end of the Empire, suggesting it remained a powerful and relevant symbol (see chapter 9).[20]

Elsewhere beyond the former Roman frontiers, torcs were reimagined as elaborate Early Medieval neck ornaments in the 5th century AD. Recent thinking suggests that at least one variety was made within the Empire to be given as diplomatic gifts to Germanic groups east of the Rhine.[21] In keeping with their different precious metal

Fig. 8.15: The chain from Traprain Law, East Lothian; NMS X.FC 248.

inheritances, these continental neck-rings tended to be made from gold. But as we have seen, Rome had relied on silver in Scotland. Its availability and its connotations of prestigious (if precarious) relationships explain why Scotland's neck ornaments are silver. Combining such a powerful material with a torc-like shape made a fitting symbol of a successful 'barbarian'–Roman political partnership or inheritance.

WHY WERE THEY BURIED IN THE GROUND?

You would notice if you lost one of these massive silver chains – we can be confident all the surviving examples had been deliberately buried rather than dropped. Burying silver objects in the ground effectively took them out of the recycling system. Given the amount of silver required for each of the chains, there must have been a powerful reason to put them out of circulation. But were they buried for safekeeping, or was the motivation more symbolic than pragmatic?

We know very little about how the chains were buried because of their accidental discovery. From what we can tell, most seem to have been found alone rather than as part of a hoard. The two exceptions are the Traprain Law and Torvean chains. Torvean [8.4] was found during construction of the Caledonian Canal in 1808, and an early newspaper report noted that 'a ball and bar also of silver' were found with it, though no further details survive.[22] The Traprain Law chain [8.15] was found on the same hillfort as both the Roman hacksilver hoard and excavated metal-working evidence (chapters 5 and 6), but on a different area of the hill subsequently destroyed by quarrying. The rest of the massive chains appear to have been single finds, some buried at wet points in the landscape. The burial of prestigious metalwork in lochs or boggy ground was a widespread and enduring tradition with deep roots that stretched back into the Bronze Age. In the centuries before the chains were made, valuable objects such as torcs were buried in wet landscapes, probably as gifts for the gods. Was this also the case for the chains?

Another factor may be the power of the chains. For a time they were the most powerful symbol of wealth and political might in the north of Britain, regalia that symbolised power over other people and land. While we lack written evidence to link the chains to individual rulers, they must have belonged to people of such status. As far as we can tell, the chains seem to be broadly contemporary with the hoards from Norrie's Law and Gaulcross, but no links or terminals survive amongst these collections of hacksilver. While brooches, dishes, pins and bangles were hacked up, the chains were not. This may have been because they were slightly earlier or later than the surviving hacksilver. But, alternatively, it may tell us that the chains were simply too politically charged to be recycled.

NOTES

1. Description from a letter (4 August 1796) accompanying the donation of the Nigg Bay chain. University of Aberdeen Museums, ABDUA 15644. Only nine links survive today.
2. Chains and discovery circumstances summarised in Youngs 2013, table 1, contra Breeze 1998.
3. This is an average of the 15 pairs of links that make up the chain body and the three enlarged end-rings: in reality the former will be lighter than the average, the latter heavier.
4. Thirty-one pairs of links survive, with a single enlarged end-ring.
5. Equivalent to a 13-inch shirt collar: Goldberg in Clarke, Blackwell and Goldberg 2012, 185.
6. National Museums Scotland unpublished report. Analysis was undertaken by Dr Susy Kirk.
7. When refashioned in 1540 it weighed 3 lb 10 oz (1.64 kg). The bonnet has since been replaced several times, most recently in 1993: Burnett and Tabraham 1993, 26–7.
8. See, for example, Clarke, Blackwell and Goldberg 2012 for a general introduction; Forsyth 1995 for the use of symbols as a formal writing system; Goldberg in preparation, on the development of the symbol corpus; Clarke and Heald 2008; Noble, Goldberg and Hamilton forthcoming, on scientific dating for the use of symbols.
9. This has been critiqued by Brian Hope-Taylor (1977, 288) and Charles Thomas (1995), amongst others.
10. Unpublished National Museums Scotland report; analysis undertaken by Dr Susy Kirk.
11. Particularly the use of sets of triple dots; Youngs 2013, 410.
12. Gavin 2013; Gavin and Newman 2007.
13. Examples of double-link copper-alloy chains include: Clickhimin, Shetland (Hamilton 1968, 82); Scatness, Shetland, estimated length 120 mm (Dockrill et al. 2015, 404, pl. 7.11.8); Gurness, Orkney (Hedges 1987, fig. 2.43); Birnie, Moray (Hunter, pers. comm.); Hurly Hawkin, Angus (Taylor 1982, 226, fig. 6.9); High Pasture Cave, Skye (Hunter forthcoming b); Dun Ardtreck, Skye (MacKie 2000, 389–90).
14. Mackie 2016, 82, fig. 4.6.
15. Evans 2000, 85–6, 384, fig. 94. The links are around 15 mm in diameter (around half the size of the massive silver chains) and the surviving length is 144 mm (around one-third of the length of the most complete silver examples).
16. Johns 1996b, 91, fig. 5.4; Charlesworth 1973.
17. See Farley and Hunter 2015, 93–6.
18. Farley and Hunter 2015, 140–1; Hunter 2010.
19. Maxfield 1981; Mráv 2015.
20. A depiction of a Roman standard-bearer with his military awards includes two small torcs worn on the chest, further linking them to the development of penannular brooches: Fig. 9.4.
21. Roymans 2017, 73.
22. *Inverness Journal*, 1 January 1808, 3.

CHAPTER NINE

Holding it together: silver and brooches

AD 400–800

The excavators, bent double over the trench, squinted to get a better look – the latest find from this hillfort in Argyll was hard to understand and very fragile. It could have been mistaken for another sherd of broken pot, but they realised it was something quite different – part of a ceramic mould made to hold and shape molten metal [Fig. 9.1]. Baked by the heat and discarded once the object had been cast, such moulds are rare finds for archaeologists. The excavations had found pieces of decorated metalwork, even a small gold mount, but this humble piece of cracked, baked clay was at least as exciting. It belonged to a substantial dump of metal-working debris which shed light on cultural connections

Fig. 9.1 (right): Ceramic mould for making a small penannular brooch with birds' heads for terminals, from Dunadd, Argyll; 33 mm (height), NMS X.1997.483.

Opposite: Detail of Clunie brooch terminal; NMS X.FC 177.

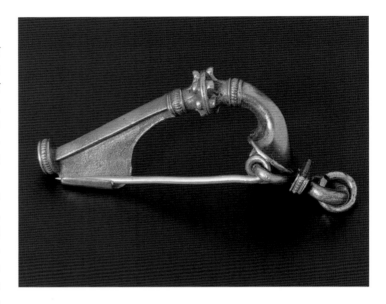

Fig. 9.2: Romano-British 'trumpet brooch' from Ayrshire. Most were copper alloy but precious examples like this were made in silver; 74mm (length), NMS X.FG 9.

with other parts of Britain and Ireland. Different types of crucible were recovered, including some used to melt and refine precious metals, while moulds showed the kinds of elaborate objects that were being produced. This hillfort, Dunadd, was a royal centre in the 7th century AD, and its smiths were making prestigious and high-quality metalwork.[1] Among these status symbols were elaborate and inventive brooches.

While silver chains had been, for a time, the epitome of status in parts of southern and north-eastern Scotland, brooches were a power symbol with a more enduring and broader appeal, made in different styles, sizes and materials, over the whole first millennium AD. Before the 7th century, brooches were just one of a range of high-status dress accessories made in silver – the pins, rings and other decorative metalwork seen in earlier chapters – but after AD 600 most surviving silver objects are brooches. For this reason they stand out, an increasingly standard medium worn to show status and power.[2]

THE BEGINNINGS OF BROOCHES

Brooch-wearing had a long history in Britain, and this influenced how Early Medieval brooches were used. They were first worn in Britain during the Iron Age, though were never very common in the north.[3] In the Roman province of *Britannia*, numbers rocketed and more styles were available to choose from. Men wore brooches singly, while women often wore them in pairs.[4] Substantial brooches secured a cloak, while smaller examples fastened lighter clothing. Some were more decorative or symbolic than functional – badges rather than brooches, often with religious symbolism.[5] The vast majority are bronze – only a small proportion are silver, and in Britain most of these are a hybrid Romano-British style, suggesting a preference for silver in *Britannia* [9.2].[6]

In the later Roman period, the choice in brooches was reduced and the popularity of a local type of fastener grew – the penannular brooch came into its own [9.3]. Used from the Iron Age and throughout the Roman period,[7] penannular brooches (with a C-shaped hoop and pin that passed through the gap and moved around the hoop to lock in place) became more popular from the 4th century, when they may have been an alternative to the crossbow brooch [5.22], used to indicate a specific social or military status.[8] Like the massive silver chains (see chapter 8), the shape of penannular brooches carried some of the symbolism of an earlier status symbol, the torc, into later fashions. Torcs,

SCOTLAND'S EARLY SILVER

Fig. 9.3: Bronze penannular brooch with stylised beast terminals, from Crichton, Midlothian; 58mm (diameter), NMS X.FT 3.

Fig. 9.4: In the Roman army, torcs were given as military awards and worn on the chest, as shown on this depiction of a Roman soldier on a gravestone from Mainz, Germany, AD 1–50. Penannular brooches evoked this symbolism. © GDKE, Landesmuseum Mainz (U. Rudischer).

originally neck ornaments, were worn on the chest as military awards in the Roman army [9.4] (page 103). The penannular brooch echoed this military symbolism – a torc-shaped object, pinned to the chest – which probably explains why they were so popular in late Roman Britain and especially in the militarised northern frontier zone.[9] These ideas, of brooches representing a particular status and being tied to military prowess, seem to have informed brooch-wearing in the centuries that followed in Scotland.[10]

New types of penannular brooch continued to be developed in the centuries after *Britannia*. Some are directly linked to Roman versions, including types with beasts' heads for terminals – creatures that face away from each other, each swallowing its own end of the hoop. A handful of these brooches were made in silver, from an example in the Gaulcross hoard, Aberdeenshire [9.5], to as far away as Lincolnshire and Wiltshire.[11] This broad but thin distribution mirrors that of other contemporary silver dress accessories, which were rarer and more widely scattered than the standard bronze versions. These silver brooches, spiral finger-rings and handpins hint at the long distance movement of élite decorated metalwork, links that stretched across 5th- to 6th-century Britain ([6.5]; see chapters 6 and 7). In this transitional period, silver objects seem to transcend ethnic and cultural boundaries to a greater degree than their bronze counterparts. Occasionally silver was imitated by coating base metal with tin, as on the minute brooch from Castlehill, Dalry, in Ayrshire [9.6].

Most early silver brooches were simple in design, with little or no additional decoration – their power came from their material and their form. The substantial brooches from the Norrie's Law and Gaulcross hoards [see 7.25] have large plain terminals, the only decorative feature being a twisted hoop.[12] Three silver brooches from a hoard at

HOLDING IT TOGETHER

Fig. 9.5 (above, left): Beast-headed brooches like this example from the Gaulcross hoard in Aberdeenshire are exceptionally rare finds in silver; 27 mm (length).

Fig. 9.6 (above, right): A tiny penannular brooch from Castlehill, Ayrshire. Made from copper alloy, the surface has been tinned to imitate silver; 21 mm (diameter), NMS X.HH 339.

Fig. 9.7 (below, left): One of three silver brooches from a hoard found at Tummel Bridge, Perthshire, in the 1880s when a storm uprooted a tree. This example has stamped decoration on its pin but is otherwise undecorated; 65 mm (diameter), NMS X.FC 163.

Fig. 9.8 (below, right): This brooch from Tummel Bridge has stamped decoration around the edges of broad terminals; 65 mm (diameter), NMS X.FC 162.

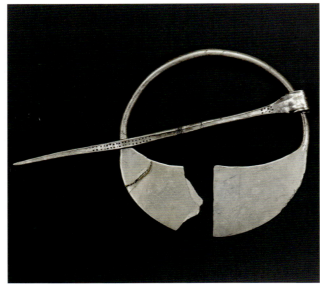

Tummel Bridge in Perthshire[13] are similarly plain – one bears a simple stamped motif on the pin [9.7], another has the same motif on even broader triangular terminals [9.8]. This brooch form was the shape of things to come – in later centuries, brooch terminals became larger, a vehicle for much more elaborate decoration.

COMPETING WITH SILVER?

The silver examined in earlier chapters – the Roman coin hoards and hacksilver (chapters 2–5), and Early Medieval massive silver chains and hacksilver hoards (chapters 8 and 9) – was found predominately in the south-east and north-east of Scotland. Here, silver clearly played an important role in élite culture and dress. There is no equivalent quantity of silver recovered from the Atlantic-facing north and west of Scotland at this time – silver objects were rare finds here during the first half of the first millennium AD [11.6].[14]

But other habits and exotic goods may have taken silver's place as a powerful way of evoking links to the legacy of the Roman world. Excavations at Whithorn in Galloway and at other power centres in Atlantic Scotland, eastern Ireland, Wales, and the south-west of England, have found small quantities of imported pottery and glass sherds dating to the late 5th and early 6th centuries AD [9.9].[15] Some of these are from Mediterranean amphorae, used to transport wine or olive oil; others from fine tablewares or glass drinking vessels. Other pottery finds include a distinctive type of vessel, the *mortarium*, which is associated with Roman-style food preparation and disproportionately well represented in Atlantic Britain and Ireland.[16] These luxury imports arrived via long-distance trading networks connected to the Aegean, north Africa and western France. The use of fine pottery and fragile glass vessels, and the consumption of olive oil or wine, were ways of evoking connections to or memories of the Roman world, an alternative to silver's *Romanitas* in eastern Scotland.[17]

This east–west split, between display through silver jewellery or consumption of imported food and drink habits, was not absolute. Very rare examples of imported pottery and glass are known from the east of Scotland, for

Fig. 9.9: Fragments from a pottery vessel made in western France, found at Dunadd, Argyll; 205mm (reconstructed height), NMS X.HPO 432, 447, 453.

HOLDING IT TOGETHER

Fig. 9.10: Part of a ceramic mould for casting a penannular brooch, from Dunadd, Argyll. Only part of the terminal survives – it was broad and would have been filled with decoration; 78 mm (height), NMS X.1997.469.

Fig. 9.11: The design for a decorated penannular brooch, scratched onto a piece of slate, from Dunadd, Argyll; 94 mm (length), NMS X.GP 218.

instance at Traprain Law[18] and at Rhynie in Aberdeenshire.[19] And connections to Roman practices could be made in other ways, including the erection of memorial stones bearing Latin inscriptions, a dozen of which have been found across southern Scotland.[20] But, generally speaking, a distinction remains, evoking connections with the Roman world through feasting in the west, and through dress, and specifically silver jewellery, in parts of the east.

RE-IMAGINING BROOCHES

From the early 7th century, both the use of silver and the popularity of brooches changed. Silver finds show that the precious metal was being used more widely across Scotland. While the objects are rare survivals, we can expand our picture by returning to the scientists. Analysis of crucibles has shown that increasing numbers are found with silver traces from the 4th–8th centuries; and they are found widely across Scotland, not just in the core areas which had controlled silver previously [11.10]. The kinds of objects made in silver also changed – while previously there had been diversity, after AD 600 the majority of surviving silver finds are brooches.

Other changes in élite culture are also apparent at this time. Pottery was still being imported, but no longer from the Mediterranean. Long-distance trade with the continent brought pottery and glass vessels, while contact with the Anglo-Saxon world brought new metalworking techniques and decorative styles. Stylistic influences from across Britain and Ireland were melded together to make a new kind of art. Art historians have labelled this creative fusion 'Insular art', a name chosen because it is a development peculiar to the islands (Latin *insulae*) of Britain and

SCOTLAND'S EARLY SILVER

Fig. 9.12: One of three brooches found near Clunie Castle, Perthshire. Unusually, this brooch is entirely silver – it does not feature gilding, an elaboration that had become standard on brooches from the 7th century; 116mm (diameter), NMS X.FC 176.

Ireland.[21] Objects made in this Insular style reimagined and combined traditional spiral-based designs (often called La Tène or Celtic art) and interlace and animal art drawn from the Germanic world. Drawing on different influences from across Britain and Ireland, Insular metalwork, sculptured stones and illuminated manuscripts were carpeted in dense and sometimes bewilderingly complex ornament. Though many of the iconic pieces of Insular art belong to the 8th century – Christian treasures like the Hilton of Cadboll cross-slab or the Lindisfarne Gospels – the roots of this hybrid style lie in élite 7th-century metalwork. Brooches provided a way of showing new connections through élite dress customs.

At Dunadd, the hillfort that produced the dump of moulds and crucibles described at the beginning of this chapter, several styles of brooch were being made at this time. One type with birds' heads for terminals, each with a large round eye and sharp, curved beak [9.1], has links to brooches found in Anglo-Saxon graves, and probably represents a fusion of the traditional penannular brooch shape with Germanic animal art. Brooches with broad terminals were also being made at Dunadd, with panels that would have been filled with decoration after casting [9.10].[22] On a piece of slate a design for this kind of brooch has been scratched into the surface of the stone, perhaps by the metalsmith who was trying out a new style [9.11]. Similar brooches were made in the east of Scotland – excavations at the hillfort of Clatchard Craig in Fife also produced moulds for casting brooches with broad, decorated terminals.[23] And both sites had access to silver: analysis of crucibles and moulds revealed traces of the precious metal, while excavations at Clatchard Craig recovered a very rare silver ingot.[24]

No finished brooches were found at either Dunadd or Clatchard Craig, only the moulds that were used to cast them. But surviving brooches elsewhere show similar designs and technology. One of three brooches from Clunie in Perthshire has the broad, expanded terminals seen in a smaller scale on the moulds. Unusually for the 7th and 8th centuries, this brooch is made from silver alone [9.12]. Other examples show how smiths incorporated new materials in their repertoire, such as gilding to highlight decorative motifs and provide visual contrast between the ornamented areas and plain silver hoops [9.13]. Gilding was new technology to Scotland, and it required new materials: gold, and the mercury necessary to bond it to the brooch's metal body.[25] In Anglo-Saxon England, gilding was often used to embellish bronze objects – making 'gold'-looking objects more widely available. In contrast,

HOLDING IT TOGETHER

Fig. 9.13: Brooch from Aldclune, Perthshire. Gilding was added to the brooch terminals and a decorative panel at the top of the hoop, creating contrast with the plain silver hoop; 65 mm (diameter), NMS X.FC 304.

Fig. 9.14: A brooch from a substantial hoard found at Rogart, Sutherland, in 1868 but mostly lost soon afterwards. The terminals, top of the hoop and pin are all decorated in chip-carved interlace, creating facets that catch the light; 78 mm (diameter), NMS X.FC 1.

in Scotland, gilding was applied to silver brooches to enrich already high-status objects.

Gilding went hand-in-hand with another key ingredient in the Insular artistic fusion: the distinctive texture of so-called 'chip-carved' designs, reminiscent of carved wood but intended to create a dazzling surface effect, with many angles helping light to catch the gilding [9.14]. Like brooch use itself, this technique had roots in Roman-period metalwork found either side of the frontier: for instance, the military belt-fittings in the Traprain Law hoard [see 5.12]. Late 5th- and 6th-century Anglo-Saxon brooches and mounts used chip-carving to create otherworldly, disconnected designs: a face here, a leg there, these motifs are almost a visual jigsaw puzzle [9.15]. During the late 6th and 7th centuries, chip-carving was used to make more coherent, complex ribbon and animal interlace designs in Anglo-Saxon and Insular metalwork, including a belt buckle from Sutton Hoo [9.16].[26] Chip-carved interlace designs became a standard way of decorating brooches in Early Medieval Scotland, with ribbon interlace looping around bosses or filling panels on the hoop or pins [9.17].

More rarely, minute strands of twisted or beaded gold wire were used on brooches to create interlacing, knotted designs [9.18]. The terminal from a brooch found at Croy [9.19] has an even more explicit link to Anglo-Saxon metalwork. Thin slabs of translucent red glass have been mounted in a framework of gold walls, imitating the garnet *cloisonné* work so prized in England.[27] This is no slavish imitation. The glass (rarer than the garnet it imitated) has been designed to fit within the local style of brooch. But Croy is not the only example of gold on a brooch made in the local style and traditional power medium of silver.

SCOTLAND'S EARLY SILVER

114

Fig. 9.15 (above, left): Early 6th-century Anglo-Saxon gilded silver brooch, from Chessell Down, Isle of Wight. Chip-carving was used in early Anglo-Saxon art to create otherworldly, disconnected designs; 138 mm (length), British Museum 1869,0729.5F.

Fig. 9.16 (above, right): Anglo-Saxon gold belt buckle. From the later 6th century, ribbon interlace designs became popular in Anglo-Saxon art. Some were plain, while others were made into writhing animals with entwined bodies and long, looping limbs. From Sutton Hoo, Suffolk; 132 mm (length), British Museum 1939,1010.1.

Fig. 9.17 (below, left): The surface of this brooch, from a hoard found at St Ninian's Isle, Shetland, is entirely covered in chip-carved interlace designs; 108 mm (diameter), NMS X.FC 284.

Fig. 9.18 (below, right): Interlace designs were also made from minute beaded gold wire. On the terminal of this brooch from Clunie, gold wire loops encircle the setting for a missing amber or glass stud. The gold wire decoration is encircled by a ring of chip-carved interlace; 36 mm (diameter), NMS X.FC 177.

HOLDING IT TOGETHER

Fig. 9.19: Silver brooch terminal from Croy, Inverness-shire, decorated with gold and glass inlays; 26 mm (terminal height), NMS X.FC 13.

Fig. 9.20 (right): The Hunterston brooch. From the front, the brooch is almost entirely covered in a thin gold veneer; 122 mm (diameter), NMS X.FC 8.

THE HUNTERSTON BROOCH

The Hunterston brooch is iconic. Holding it, one is struck by its size and weight, and by the richness of its decoration. It is the most intricately decorated piece of Early Medieval metalwork ever found in Scotland. The front is sumptuous, almost entirely covered in a rich golden carpet of fine filigree decoration [9.20]. This is usually how people encounter it, displayed in a museum gallery or illustrated in books. But the brooch is a double-sided object, and turning it over reveals this golden face to be a thin veneer built on a solid silver body. The back is also decorated – there is more to the Hunterston brooch than meets the eye. This is a brooch that was meant to be handled as well as worn.

The Hunterston brooch was made in the late 7th century. Its front bears new designs, created using new metalworking technology, rendered in a new material – gold. Thin gold foils carry minute gold filigree wire and granules, worked into contorting, twisting animals and interlacing ribbons. The centre of the brooch terminals cage tiny upside-down creatures with sinewy bodies and long snouts made from gold wire less than 0.3 mm thick [9.21]. In the smaller panels surrounding these intimidating yet miniature beasts are more abstract creatures: single interlacing strands with only the merest hint of a head, an eye or a tail [9.22]. These ribbon-like creatures were not part of existing metalworking traditions in Scotland or Ireland. Instead, the animals – and the technology and material which created them – are the product of links to the Anglo-Saxon world.[28] Gold ruled supreme within the Anglo-Saxon kingdoms – by the 7th century, earlier varied styles combining gold with silver had been replaced by a homogenous élite aesthetic based on gold and semi-precious garnets. Treasures of the Anglo-Saxon world, such as the weapons and dress fittings from the royal burials at Sutton Hoo in the kingdom of East Anglia, show a masterful combination of interlace and animal art, gold and garnet [see 9.16].

SCOTLAND'S EARLY SILVER

Fig. 9.21: The Hunterston brooch features fearsome creatures made from fine beaded gold wire. The way the creatures have been made and mounted onto gold sheet shows connections to Anglo-Saxon metalwork; NMS X.FC 8.

Fig. 9.22: Gold wire was also used to make subtle snake-like creatures on the front of the Hunterston brooch; NMS X.FC 8.

Though there are no garnet insets on the Hunterston brooch,[29] gold and interlacing animal designs have taken centre stage. And though, as we've seen, other brooches from Scotland had used small amounts of gold, the front of the Hunterston brooch signals a departure in the prominence and extent of its golden decoration. The jeweller who made it masterfully combined different artistic influences in a way that defines the art of this period in Britain and Ireland. This fusion is so accomplished that it is impossible to trace objects back to the places they were made. It is far from certain that the Hunterston brooch was manufactured within Early Medieval Scotland. The closest surviving example is from Ireland, the so-called 'Tara' brooch; the two brooches share the same form and mixture of motifs, materials and technology. Neither can be pinned down to a place of manufacture.

Turning the brooch over, its appearance is very different [9.23]. Underneath all the gold, the body is made from silver, the material that had been the ultimate symbol of power in Scotland for hundreds of years. While the front has a uniform golden colour and texture, the back is more complicated – silver is combined with gold, undecorated metal is punctuated with panels of cast decoration, motifs with very different pedigrees are combined. The golden front bears only interlacing designs; but on the other side, panels of ribbon interlace and entwined animals are juxtaposed with motifs with a long heritage stretching back into the Roman Iron Age [9.24]. Based on patterns of spirals, the only place these traditional designs appear is on the back, floating in a sea of silver. But though the spiral designs have deep roots, the motifs have been reimagined, and their meaning as well as their shape had shifted over time. Sets of these spiral patterns also appear on Christian sculptured stones in Pictland [9.25], worked into arrangements that contain hidden representations of the Cross. Each of the spirals is made from three interlocking arms, which on a Christian monument must reference the holy Trinity of Father, Son and Spirit.

HOLDING IT TOGETHER

Fig. 9.23 (left): From the back, it is clear that the Hunterston brooch is made from silver. Panels of gilt decoration show that it was meant to be seen from both sides. These panels – **Fig. 9.24, below** – contain spiral decoration, the only place this traditional motif is found on the brooch; NMS X.FC 8.

Fig. 9.25 (foot of page): Traditional spiral motifs were reimagined in early Christian art and combined into complex panels of swirling and interlocking designs on carved stones, as on the Hilton of Cadboll cross slab; NMS X.IB 189.

POWERFUL BROOCHES

The Hunterston brooch encapsulates a mixture of old and new, local and international, reconciled – beautifully – in silver and gold. But what kind of power did this most spectacular of brooches represent? By the time it was made written sources speak of recognisable kingdoms within Scotland. It is easy to see it as a brooch fit for a king, but political power had also gained a new dimension. More than a belief system, Christianity had brought new ways to wield and legitimise power, both practically through the gifting of land to create networks of monasteries, and symbolically through links forged between divine and kingly authority. Insular art tends to be associated with a golden age of early Christianity that founded monasteries capable of producing exceptional manuscripts, sculpture and metalwork. But the roots of this hybrid art style are

SCOTLAND'S EARLY SILVER

Fig. 9.26 (below): Brooches were made in a wide range of sizes in Early Medieval Scotland. Amongst the smallest is this fragment of a penannular brooch from Freswick Links, Caithness, which would have been only around 25mm in diameter when complete; NMS X.IL 654.

Fig 9.27 (right): Among the hoard of twelve brooches from St Ninian's Isle, Shetland, are a group almost identical in size. One brooch, lacking its pin, is substantially bigger than the others; 108mm in diameter rather than 71mm, NMS X.FC 284–95.

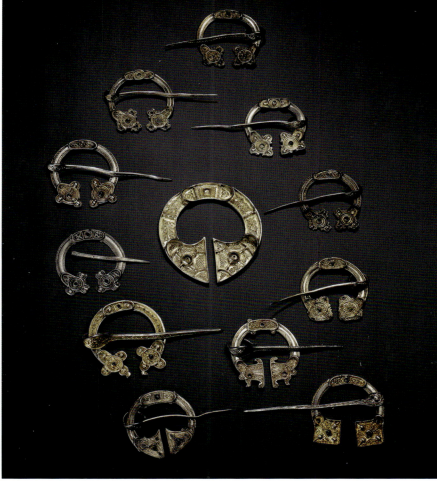

more complicated, embedded in royal networks and kingly power centres. Early artistic experimentation recognised in the finds from hillforts like Dunadd, Argyll, and the Mote of Mark, Galloway, was made possible by the wider connections and politics of powerful people in Early Medieval Scotland.[30] But it also grew out of their need to create new, unifying, power symbols for kingdoms forged from what had previously been competing territories.[31] All in all, it is difficult to unravel secular and religious might in this period, but silver was a key medium in demonstrating this power.

Hunterston is the most grand and most sumptuous brooch to survive, but other examples illustrate the range in scale and grandeur of Early Medieval clothes-fasteners: one of the smallest, from Freswick Links, was only around 25mm in diameter [9.26]. The hoard from St Ninian's Isle, Shetland contains a suite of silver brooches [9.27]. Though they vary in decoration, most are similar in size: seven have a maximum diameter of 7.1cm (within 1mm), perhaps suggesting that they were all modelled from the same example.[32] Moulds excavated at the Brough of Birsay on Orkney show the manufacture of much smaller versions of this style of brooch [9.28, 9.29].

HOLDING IT TOGETHER

Fig. **9.28:** Brooch from St Ninian's Isle, Shetland; NMS X.FC 288.

Fig. **9.29:** Ceramic mould for casting a penannular brooch, from Brough of Birsay, Orkney. The mould would have made a smaller version of brooches found in the St Ninian's Isle hoard; 71mm (length), NMS X.HB 298.

It is tempting to allot these brooches to different levels of society – from the richest for princes to more modest examples for their followers. But in fact we have very little evidence for who wore brooches in Early Medieval Scotland. Anglo-Saxon beliefs meant that people were buried fully clothed, and while the placement of objects in the grave may not exactly mirror practices during life, these burials provide a good indication of broad dress styles and customs. In Scotland, by and large people buried their dead without objects – perhaps in shrouds rather than clothed. This means that we know far less about dress habits in Scotland (and Ireland and Wales) than in the Anglo-Saxon areas. In England, grave evidence from the 5th–7th centuries tells us that brooches were generally worn by women. A much later Irish law tract makes provision for brooches to be worn in Ireland by both men and women, and describes different brooches tied to ranks in society, though it may be as late as the 11th or 12th century.[33] Scotland has neither surviving burials nor written sources about dress, status and brooch use, though there are a few depictions of brooch-wearing on early Christian sculptured stones. Where it is possible to determine, these brooch users seem to be women, but whether these images reflect daily practice or recurring Christian symbolism (perhaps connected to the Virgin) remains unclear. The Hunterston brooch, exceptional in so many ways, stands out here – uniquely it carries the name of someone who owned it, albeit several hundred years after it was made.

SCOTLAND'S EARLY SILVER

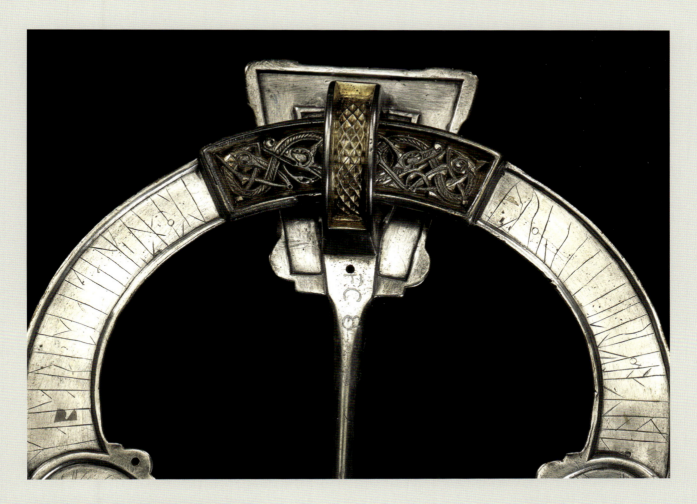

CLAIMING THE HUNTERSTON BROOCH

On the front of the brooch, every available surface is covered in ornament. There is simply no free space – beasts and scrolls, amber and gold, are crammed into every nook and cranny. The back of the brooch originally had some clear water – stretches of undecorated silver in between islands of decoration. But not any more. Several centuries after the brooch was made, someone filled in the blanks. An inscription was scratched onto the plain silver hoop, written in stick-like runes [9.30]. It reads 'Malbriþa á stilk', usually translated as 'Malbriþa owns [this] brooch'.[34] The runes are Scandinavian but the name is Gaelic – Máel Brigte or 'servant of Brigid' – and its rendering might suggest a local dialect, perhaps in a mixed-language community.[35]

The rest of the empty silver around the inscription was also filled with rune-like decoration, scratched lines, some of which are legible runes, but most of which are not. This looks very much like a way of filling up the page, leaving no room for anyone else to come along and add their name.[36] Perhaps this decoration was a fail-safe against a rival claim for ownership?

Fig. 9.30: Several centuries after it was made, someone staked a late claim of ownership on the Hunterston brooch. A runic inscription has been scratched around part of the hoop, and the rest of the undecorated silver filled with rune-like decoration; NMS X.FC 8.

HOLDING IT TOGETHER

Fig. 9.31 (below): Part of a penannular brooch, from the hoard found at Croy, Inverness-shire; 88mm (height), NMS X.FC 14.

Fig. 9.32 (right): The Croy hoard, comprising incomplete brooches, Anglo-Saxon silver coins, beads, a length of fine silver-wire chain and part of a balance beam used for weighing; 108mm (brooch diameter), NMS X.FC 12–25.

The Hunterston brooch is in remarkably good condition. By the time the runic inscription was scratched on the back, the brooch may already have been a two-hundred-year-old antique. But there are no signs that it was in the process of being taken to pieces. A few insets have been lost but, generally speaking, the extremely fragile gold decoration survives well. And it is whole – this brooch was never conceived as hacksilver. Though its meaning will have changed as it passed through different pairs of hands, thankfully it was never valued only as bullion. If it had been, either during the Early Medieval period or when it was found in the 19th century, it may not have survived until today. In contrast, brooches in the Croy hoard [9.31][37] were hacked up. Coins and a balance beam for weighing from the hoard suggest it was buried in the late 9th century [9.32]. Though some of the objects are local status symbols, this was a hoard buried by someone who hacked silver and traded using standard weights. The Vikings had arrived in Scotland.

SCOTLAND'S EARLY SILVER

122

NOTES

1. This description evokes the most recent excavations at Dunadd, carried out in 1980–81 (Lane and Campbell 2000). Finds included crucibles used for melting silver and gold (*ibid.*, table 5.5) and moulds for casting a variety of fine decorated metalwork, including bird-headed brooches (*ibid.*, 114–8; illustrated example [9.1] is cat. no. 1098). Silver was detected in one mould, for the production of an Anglo-Saxon-style buckle component (*ibid.*, 127–9, illus. 4.32, 4.35, SF298).
2. Other silver objects are known from Early Medieval Scotland, though few survive. In addition to the silver buckle component mould from Dunadd, a silver pin from Kilellan also shows Anglo-Saxon influence in the choice of garnet for inlays and in the form of the pin (Ritchie 2005, 143–4). The 8th-century hoard of silver objects from St Ninian's Isle, Shetland, includes bowls, a spoon and fork-like object, weapon-fittings and mounts, alongside a collection of brooches. Descriptions of a lost hoard of silver found in the 1880s at the Broch of Burgar, Orkney, include silver vessels, combs, pins, chains and brooches, as well as amber beads (Graham-Campbell 1985). Graham-Campbell concluded it was most likely to have been a hoard of Pictish silver buried around AD 800, though it may alternatively have been Viking Age given the description of the silver vessel (now paralleled by the Galloway hoard) and the silver comb (paralleled by a sole example from the hoard of Viking Age silver from Cuerdale, Lancashire; Graham-Campbell 2013). The Viking Age hoard from Talnotrie, Galloway, also includes late Anglo-Saxon silver pins and a strap end (Webster and Backhouse 1991, 273–4).
3. Hunter 2009 c.
4. Johns 1996 b.
5. Allason-Jones 2014.
6. Silver examples account for around 0.2% of the total Roman brooches included in the Portable Antiquities Scheme database for England (25,857 copper alloy, 62 silver, 3 gold). [www.finds.org.uk – accessed 24/8/17]
7. Fowler 1960; Booth 2015.
8. Collins 2010, 73.
9. Maxfield 1981; Goldberg 2015 a, 165, fig. 56; Laing 1994, 24.
10. Nieke (1993) explored the role of Early Medieval brooches as status symbols and links back to Roman practices and sumptuary legislation that limited the wearing of particular object types and materials in the Empire.
11. Two silver zoomorphic penannular brooches are known from the northern frontier from Littlethorpe and Piercebridge (Collins 2010, 77). Two further silver examples are recorded within the Portable Antiquities Scheme database: SWYOR-EC09E8 from Kirton in Lindsey in North Lincolnshire; and WILT-809E32 from Cherhill in Wiltshire. A single silver example decorated with enamel is known from Caistor, Lincolnshire (Youngs 2009, 57, fig. 16).
12. Neither now has a pin. Laing suggested these hoops were Roman military awards in the shape of brooches, rather than functioning fasteners (Laing 1994, 24).
13. The hoard was found in the 1880s in the roots of a tree that had been blown down (Anon. 1888). As well as the brooches, fragmentary bronze hanging-bowl mounts and parts of a bronze vessel were also recovered (Bruce-Mitford 2005, 323–7).
14. A number of factors, including acidic soils, a cultural avoidance of hoard deposits, and different levels of excavation and metal-detecting, may have affected the picture of silver in the west of Scotland, but it is just as likely that different areas of Scotland were behaving in different ways. The distribution of surviving silver objects and evidence for precious metalworking is considered further in the Conclusion.
15. Campbell 2007.
16. *Ibid.*, 27; there has been considerable debate over the function of these vessels and whether they were linked to the adoption of Roman cuisine (see Cool 2006, 42–6).
17. The presence at Dunadd and a handful of other sites in Britain of a particular type of imported vessel (*mortaria*, in a fabric known as DSPA) has been highlighted as 'indicating the presence

of people there with memories of, or aspirations to, a Roman type of lifestyle' (Campbell 2007, 27).
18. Ingemark 2014, 78–81.
19. Noble et al 2013, 1142.
20. See Forsyth 2005.
21. Goldberg 2015a.
22. Lane and Campbell 2000, 118–9, cat. no. 1636, illus. 4.19, 4.20.
23. Close-Brooks 1986, fig. 22.
24. Lane and Campbell 2000, table 5.5; Close-Brooks 1986, 167.
25. Mercury gilding (also known as fire gilding) was used to gild Early Medieval bronze and silver. Gold was mixed with mercury to form an amalgam, applied to the surface of the object and heated, causing the mercury to volatilise and leaving behind a layer of gold chemically bonded to the surface.
26. Another find from Sutton Hoo comprises chip-carved bridle mounts, and moulds for making similar objects were found at Mote of Mark in Kirkcudbrightshire (Laing and Longley 2006, 148–51).
27. Garnet-bearing objects were analysed in 2016 as part of a project by the Römisch-Germanisches Zentralmuseum in Mainz, Germany, to provenance the Early Medieval gemstones. This confirmed that the insets in the Croy brooch are glass rather than garnets (Alex Hilgner, pers. comm.).
28. Niamh Whitfield has studied the filigree of both the Hunterston and 'Tara' brooches in considerable detail. She concludes that both show many similarities in design and technology to Anglo-Saxon metalwork, whilst recognising small but significant differences. See, for example, Whitfield 1993; 1997; 2007; 2013.
29. Some of the missing stones could have been garnet or a glass imitation – contemporary brooches from Westness and the Croy hoard feature translucent red glass, and garnet jewellery was being recycled at fine metalworking centres like Dunadd and perhaps the Brough of Birsay, which produced a stray slab of garnet (Curle 1982, 122, no. 648).
30. Lane and Campbell 2000; Laing and Longley 2006.
31. Campbell 2009.
32. Small, Thomas and Wilson 1973. The incomplete nature of the brooch pins makes comparing the weights of these brooches difficult, but the variation between those with a complete pin (54.5 g–68.3 g) is too great to suggest that weight rather than size was important. One brooch was markedly larger: its hoop alone weighs 149.7 g. For comparison, the other brooches in the hoard weigh between 39.7 g–98.5 g (Small, Thomas and Wilson 1973, 67–79).
33. Whitfield 2001; 2004; Etchingham and Swift 2004.
34. Barnes and Page 2006, 217–21. The inscription is literally 'malbriþaastilk'. The rendering of the personal name may suggest a local dialect, perhaps in a mixed language community. The word 'stilkr' meant either stem or stalk, but could also mean pin, and in this context most likely refers to the brooch itself. An alternative reading includes 'stilk' as a byname, giving 'Malbiþa stilk owns [me, this]', but most commentators are content with the primary reading. The inscription cannot be more closely dated than a couple of centuries later than the making of the brooch, which is usually placed between AD 650–750.
35. Barnes and Page 2006, 220.
36. Youngs 1989, 92.
37. Only two coins were found and both had been perforated for use as jewellery, meaning they provide a less strong basis for dating the deposition of the hoard than other Viking Age deposits. A notional deposition date of around 845 has been suggested: Blackburn and Pagan 1986, no. 51.

9.33: Silver-gilt penannular brooch, St Ninian's Isle; 71mm (diameter), NMS X.FC 295.

HOLDING IT TOGETHER

CHAPTER TEN
New sources and new ideas
AD 800–1000

GREEN SILVER – THE ST NINIAN'S ISLE HOARD, SHETLAND

The silver bowls, brooches and fittings gleamed brightly one last time as the box was closed and hastily buried underneath the cross-marked slab. That glint would fade over the next thousand years. When the St Ninian's Isle hoard was discovered in 1958 under the floor of a Medieval church on a Shetland island, the objects were so covered in verdigris (green-coloured copper corrosion) they looked as though they were made from copper.[1] In many cases the original metal was so debased that it actually contained more copper than silver. Intensive restoration has brought most of these objects back to their former silvery glory, but some were too far gone. They reveal their debased silver content through rippling green corrosion, like frozen shock waves reverberating across the surface [Fig. 10.1].

Over the four hundred years since Roman imperial supplies had ceased in the 5th century AD, silver had been gradually debased, mostly through dilution with copper alloys. It had remained vital as the base material for the highest calibre of brooches, but these symbols of power and status in the 7th and 8th centuries AD laid greater emphasis on artistry, an eclectic repertoire of ornament, and embellishment with a range of materials, rather than the lavish use of large amounts of silver. Small amounts of gold were used as gilding or for inset filigree panels, while coloured glass and amber settings added flashes of colour [10.2; see chapter 9]. The clearest indicator of the dilution of silver quality by the 8th century AD comes from scientific analysis of the St Ninian's Isle hoard, which shows silver debased in some cases to less than 50% purity.[2] These

Fig. 10.1 (opposite): Two bowls from the St Ninian's Isle hoard, tainted green by copper corrosion; 145 mm (diameter), NMS X.FC 270 and 272.

Fig. 10.2: Detail of a gilded and enamelled mount in the base of a bowl from the St Ninian's Isle hoard; NMS X.FC 273.

Fig. 10.3: The St Ninian's Isle hoard; NMS X.FC 268–96.

debased brooches, bowls and fittings would have looked more silvery than they really were – it seems that looks were more important than purity at this time [10.3].

The burial of the St Ninian's Isle hoard is often linked to the threat of Vikings. There is no concrete evidence to confirm this, although the earliest accounts of Viking raids suggest they targeted monasteries and key Christian sites such as Iona and Lindisfarne at the very end of the 8th century AD. This was just a prelude to the story of a new age of silver – the Viking Age.

NEW SOURCES OF WEALTH: SILVER AND SLAVES

The advent of the Viking Age brought great changes in the supply of silver to Scotland, the objects being made, and the fortunes of their owners.

We see a dramatic increase in silver objects from the 9th century onwards. Hacksilver hoards reappeared in the archaeological record after a hiatus of several centuries (chapter 7).[3] Viking Age hoards often mixed coinage and ingots, whole objects and hacked ones, just like the earlier hacksilver hoards [10.4].[4] In some ways they look very similar: they offer clear evidence of a silver bullion economy, with the destruction of previous fashions and objects, the hacking of valued material by weight, and its burial. But there are significant differences. New connections to continental and Near Eastern sources became available through

Fig. 10.4 (below): Viking Age hacksilver – the Storr Rock hoard, Skye; NMS X.IL 282–304.

Fig. 10.5 (right, above): Islamic coins (*dirhams*) from the Storr Rock hoard; 25 mm (diameter).

Fig. 10.6 (right, below): Anglo-Saxon coins from the Storr Rock hoard; 22 mm (diameter).

Scandinavia and across the North Sea, not from southern routes to the Mediterranean as before. These new supplies included *dirhams* [10.5], a type of coinage from the Islamic world, produced to a high standard of purity and part of transcontinental trade up the Russian rivers from the Black Sea to the Baltic and beyond. Russia is named after the Rus, a group of Scandinavian origin who dominated this riverine trade from the Near East to northern Europe. Coins from Anglo-Saxon kingdoms were another source of silver in Scottish Viking Age hoards, as no king in Scotland minted coins until the 12th century [10.6; pp. 3–5].[5]

NEW SOURCES AND NEW IDEAS

If new supplies of silver moved across the North Sea from Scandinavia to Britain and Ireland, what resources travelled in the opposite direction? What was exchanged? Silver was used in trade and transactions; it is often a proxy for other things and other forms of wealth. So what did silver buy? Early Medieval Irish laws mention various units of value including a *cumal* and a *sét*. In origin, *cumal* meant 'female slave' but was also used as a term for an established weight of silver. *Sét* meant 'treasure, jewel, valuable'; it was used in the Irish legal system of fines and to express the honour-price of ranks below the level of king. Although the relative value of these things would have changed at different times, a general equation was made between 1 milch cow = 1 ounce of silver = 2 *séts* = 1/3 *cumal*. A female slave was worth three cattle or 3 ounces' weight in silver.[6]

This relationship between silver and slaves should come as no great surprise – human traffic has been bought and sold for silver throughout history. The human impact of the Viking Age is often sought in the people who came to Scotland from Scandinavia, those that we can see in the archaeological record through burials lavishly equipped with objects. But the greater impact was on those who left: the human traffic of slavery that sailed away against their will from these shores, bought with silver. Slavery undoubtedly existed before the Viking Age, but the visible presence of silver in coinage, bullion and hacksilver, and the boom in silver hoards, are archaeological indicators of increased wealth, measured not just in silver but in slaves.[7]

SECURITY AND STATUS: THE SOCIAL USES OF SILVER

The furnished burial tradition of the 9th and 10th centuries practised by Scandinavian incomers and their kinfolk allows us snapshots of how people may have appeared in life, or at least how their relatives wanted the final view of them. They were buried with objects of use and value, both Scandinavian-style items and local heirloom pieces.[8] Some of these burials were placed near older monuments or earlier graveyards, continuing a theme we have seen at various times over the first millennium AD where new expressions of power sought connections with the past.

Some Viking Age hoards were also buried near older monuments, especially in the Orkney Isles.[9] The burial of hoards in the Viking Age is usually seen as an indicator of a lack of security; arguments about whether these were deposited at prominent places in the landscape so they could be reclaimed or whether they may have been sacrificed as offerings are rarely rehearsed for this period (compare the interpretation of the earlier hoards from Norrie's Law and Gaulcross; pp. 91–2).[10] By far the largest such hoard in Britain is Cuerdale, from Lancashire [10.14], buried around AD 900 and often linked to the expulsion of Scandinavian settlers from Dublin, who then moved elsewhere around the Irish Sea.[11] The biggest silver hoard from Scotland, found at Skaill in Orkney (buried around AD 950–70), shows how fashions changed quickly over the 10th century.[12] It included new styles of object compared to the earlier Viking Age silver hoards – notably new hybrid styles of penannular brooch, such as the so-called thistle brooch [10.7] which combined an Irish and British form

with Scandinavian design. These were very popular in the Irish Sea zone, and influenced new fashions of jewellery in Scandinavia. Thistle brooches and another hybrid form, bossed penannular brooches [10.8], were new takes on well-established dress accessories in Britain and Ireland that were re-imagined for a new age, drawing on new forms of ornament from Scandinavia.[13]

Personal wealth could be expressed in these dress-fasteners and other items of jewellery, as could clientage, the ability to command other people. Brooches were already established as a means of gift exchange before the Viking Age – this probably explains why Anglo-Saxon and Pictish terms for brooch were borrowed into Old Irish.[14] Clientage was also expressed through the vast numbers of arm-rings that would have been given to clients by their leaders. These have often been explored in purely economic terms, with a focus on weights and value, but we should always remember that the objects which survive are proxies for people, and act as a gateway into a richer and more personal view of the past. Brooches pinned clothing in place; arm-rings were proudly worn on the wrist; both items could be given as pledges or gifts by the rich to ensure support from their followers. A hoard of arm-rings [10.9] signifies the ability to command a large number of men, perhaps a war band – they could have been accumulated from defeated war bands and either redistributed or re-made into new fashions.[15]

These new objects of the Viking Age, especially arm-rings, are signals of the portability of wealth. They also

Fig. 10.7 (above, left): Thistle brooch from the Skaill hoard, Orkney – a new style of penannular brooch typical of the Viking Age; 154mm (diameter), NMS X.IL 742.

Fig. 10.8 (above, right): Bossed penannular brooch from the Galloway hoard; 78mm (diameter).

NEW SOURCES AND NEW IDEAS

Fig. 10.9 a and b (left and below): Arm-rings (so-called ring-money) from the Burray hoard, Orkney; c.70 mm (diameter), X.IL 236–67, 270–1 (selection).

Fig. 10.10 (opposite, left): Ingots and folded arm-rings from the Galloway hoard.

Fig. 10.11 (opposite, right): Unusual finds of a gold bird-pin, gold bracelet, ornate glass beads, Anglo-Saxon silver brooches and strap fittings and decorated Viking arm-ring; 74 mm (pin length).

show regional variation and responses to local traditions. So-called ring-money, penannular arm-rings of simple undecorated form, is common in Scotland (especially in the Hebrides and Northern Isles), while broad-band arm-rings are much more common in the Irish-Sea zone (see page 133).[16] Ring-money was developed after the early period of furnished burial – none were worn in those graves.[17] Arm-rings show no single Scandinavian tradition but a series of regional responses, while the brooches discussed above mixed local and Scandinavian styles. The decoration may be new and Scandinavian, but the form of the brooch represented modes of dress and appearance that had been established in Scotland for nearly a thousand years. The material – silver – had been the primary means of expressing wealth and power since it was first introduced from the Roman world hundreds of years earlier, but such lavish use of silver had not been possible since the massive silver chains and the abundant supplies of raw material those singular items signify. The substantial Viking Age dress accessories are a visible sign of the fresh supplies of silver. The increase in hoarding in the Viking Age is also testament to those new supplies of silver, refreshing a centuries-old tradition.

SCOTLAND'S EARLY SILVER

THE GALLOWAY HOARD

The Galloway Hoard, found in 2014, is the richest collection of rare and unique Viking Age objects ever found in Britain or Ireland.

Buried around AD 900, the bulk of the hoard is Viking-period silver – ingots and arm-rings typical of the Irish Sea region but, until now, rare in Scotland [10.10]. This silver had been converted to bullion – folded and flattened, or melted down into easily transportable blocks. The hoard also contains rare and exotic items from the Anglo-Saxon world, the Holy Roman and Byzantine Empires, and beyond.

The hoard was buried in two distinct layers. First to be unearthed was a cache of 11 silver ingots, 11 silver arm-rings, and a rare silver-gilt Christian cross. This may have acted as a decoy for a larger deposit buried deeper underneath which contained twice as many flattened silver arm-rings and ingots as the upper deposit. There was also a bundle of intact silver arm-rings around the remains of a small wooden box with three rare gold objects – an ingot, a unique bird-shaped pin, and a ring nestled inside. But the highlight of this lower deposit was a silver-gilt vessel packed full of the rarest and most precious treasures, including amulets of glass and rock crystal, various types of silver brooches, Anglo-Saxon silver mounts and another gold ingot [10.11]. Inside this hoard-within-a-hoard-within-a-hoard were further surprises – objects preserved in their original textile wrappings. These are still to be fully revealed but appear to comprise three socketed gold terminals (perhaps jewelled manuscript pointers known as *aestels*) in one bundle, and a second parcel containing a gold-mounted carved rock crystal object wrapped in silk.

There is a lot of work still to do – the hoard requires significant conservation and research before we can fully understand its contents. But the future is exciting – unlocking its secrets has the potential to reveal new insights into the Viking Age world, to understand its people and their stories and connections.

NEW SOURCES AND NEW IDEAS

10.12 (left): Viking brooch, neck-ring and arm-ring from the Skaill hoard.

10.13 (right): Detail of Anglo-Saxon brooch from the Galloway hoard.

NOTES

1. For the hoard, see Small, Thomas and Wilson 1973; Clarke 2008.
2. McKerrell 1973.
3. Though individual finds of apparently hacked-up brooches indicate that hacking of silver had continued over this period; see Small, Thomas and Wilson 1973, pl. XXXVIIb, XXXVIII, XLIVb; *Discovery and Excavation in Scotland* 2007, 96.
4. Graham-Campbell 1995.
5. See essays in Graham-Campbell and Williams 2007.
6. Kelly 2005, 112–16.
7. Barrett 2008.
8. Graham-Campbell and Batey 1998.
9. Graham-Campbell 1995, 60.
10. See discussion in Grane 2013, 369.
11. Graham-Campbell 2013.
12. Graham-Campbell 1995, 34–48.
13. Graham-Campbell 2013, 112–7.
14. Etchingham and Swift 2004.
15. Barrett 2007, 318; Critch 2015.
16. Sheehan 2013; Graham-Campbell 1995, 38–40.
17. Graham-Campbell and Batey 1998, 113–54.

SCOTLAND'S EARLY SILVER

Fig. 10.14: The Cuerdale hoard, discovered in Lancashire in 1840, is still the largest hacksilver hoard from Britain and Ireland. It weighs c.42.6 kilograms. From the British Museum.

NEW SOURCES AND NEW IDEAS

CHAPTER ELEVEN

Conclusion: a thousand years of silver

Silver should have been a useless metal. You didn't need it. It didn't make better ploughs or pots, sharper knives or warmer homes. But it was rare and exotic, and reflected light with a dazzling intensity that few other materials could. Such factors gave it enormous potency as a symbol of power, prestige and connections.

There are many ways to show off. At different times and places, people in ancient Scotland showed their power and aspirations through substantial architecture, stone monuments, feasting, the possession of cattle, or elaborate jewellery made from bronze, gold, glass or jet. The arrival of silver opened another avenue for marking or claiming prestige, and one which showed powerful connections. Scotland's early silver was all imported. Acquiring it took effort and contacts, whether through relationships with foreign powers or links to people who already had it.[1] Using silver made these connections obvious to others, and this was part of its attraction.

Two thousand years ago, silver was a new metal in what is now Scotland, brought from distant lands by the Roman army. The ways it was used changed over time – and also changed the people who owned, made, handled or were impressed by it. We have tried to tell the story of the key steps in its history over a thousand years. Now we step back to seek a broader view. What did silver do for and to people in the first millennium AD in this area? How did its use change? What did silver mean to people so long ago?

SILVER IN CHANGING TIMES

There was a fundamental difference between the first local use of silver in Scotland and what came next. This first

Opposite: Hacksilver from the Traprain Treasure.

Fig. 11.1: Roman *denarii* from the Falkirk hoard; NMS X.FR 482.

Fig. 11.2: Roman hacksilver from Traprain Law; NMS X.GVA 4.

phase was short-lived but had dramatic impacts. A few Roman items reached local hands in the 1st and 2nd centuries AD, but it was the flood of silver coins in the late 2nd century AD, especially into central and eastern Scotland, which provoked big social changes [Fig. 11.1].[2] These were diplomatic gifts intended by the Romans to buy peace on the northern frontier. To Iron Age communities in Scotland coins were a new type of object, made from a new metal, bearing unfamiliar images. They could not be spent here, beyond the Empire's edge – but they were not treated just as money. Silver coins were special. In local status-conscious societies, they were transformed from economic tool to power symbol – not by melting them down and recycling them, as might seem obvious to us, but by giving them new meaning as prestige items. These silver coins symbolised the owner's status and connections. And these same connections proved disastrous, as Rome used *denarii* to create discord and dependency, building up some groups at the expense of others and then pulling away the supply. This was a fast-burn, high-impact phenomenon. Powerful groups quickly reacted to the availability of silver – it became a vital part of their prestige – but it ultimately contributed to the collapse of their political systems.

Later use was much more engaged and involved. From the late 3rd century on, silver was no longer simply admired and used as it came – it was a raw material transformed to local needs and desires. The source was still Roman, but now in the form of bullion rather than coin [11.2]. In the late 3rd–early 5th century, silver vessels, spoons and other items were cut to set weights and passed north in return for services rendered, whether fighting for Rome or agreeing to keep the peace.[3] Now silver acquired a real local role. It was embedded in local politics, a vital ingredient in local recipes of power, manipulated, diluted or enhanced as required.

Fig. 11.3: Massive silver chains.

For the first time, this Roman bullion was transformed into local jewellery on a variety of scales.[4] Most were small and subtle personal items – finger-rings, pins, quite modest brooches, and rare grooming items like tweezers. Silver will catch the eye at a distance, but details would require up-close scrutiny, and decoration, if any, was also small and subtle. Material, not ornament, was key in using this new substance. Many were silver versions of items normally made in bronze – the new material made them special. This focus on silver as a material spurred attempts to emulate it, fooling the onlooker with coatings of tin over a cheaper bronze base.

Most striking of all were the massive silver neckchains, so different in scale from other jewellery of the time that they may have represented regalia in a world of emergent small-scale kingdoms [11.3].[5] These chains epitomise the desire to show off through mass of material rather than ornate ornament – only two are decorated, but all are visually dominant from their sheer mass. Quantity, not subtlety, was key. Unlike the other silver jewellery, these had no obvious bronze equivalents, though they evoked both earlier Iron Age power symbols and those of the late Roman army. But was it the owner's own power that they showed, or their social role? And who wore such objects? For rings, pins and brooches we have no evidence – but the size of some chains indicates it was women or youths, not men, that they adorned.

These chains show how much silver was available in Scotland. Research into two hacksilver hoards whose contents span the end of Roman Britain is revealing how silver from the Roman world was managed and reused in the following centuries.[6] Both hoards, from Norrie's Law in Fife and Gaulcross in Aberdeenshire, contain well-known and widespread types of objects as well as rare survivals. Many fragments remain unparalleled or unidentified, but others show items – elements of a helmet, parts of a bowl – which are otherwise lost to us. Recycling has been so thorough throughout history that these rare ancient caches provide the only snapshot of objects on the verge of re-melting, fragments of things once prized for their form or decoration, but only valued for their weight of material when they were buried.

Personal ornaments dominated early silver use. Wearing silver was a highly visible signalling of status or power,

CONCLUSION

139

Fig. 11.4: Early Medieval silver brooch with gold and amber inlays, Westness, Orkney; 55mm (diameter), NMS X.IL 728.

linked directly to a person's body and being, observed in their very actions. It seems you wore your prestige. But over time the range of silver ornaments narrowed markedly. Where once rings, torcs, brooches, arm ornaments and pins were made, from around AD 600 brooches dominated.[7] Variants of the long-lived penannular form, these brooches were tailored in size, ornament and material for different users according to their age, sex, status and connections. The silver used to make them was diluted to make it go further – suggesting purity was less of an issue than visual effect, as quite a lot of copper can be added to the mix before it becomes visually tainted. But silver alone was no longer enough by the 7th century. It was augmented with thin coatings of gold and colourful inlays of glass, amber and garnet. New connections with the Anglo-Saxon world caused people in Scotland to adapt, creating hybrid styles of objects and using new metalworking technologies and motifs [11.4]. This was a time when powerful people sought to rule over larger areas, over-riding old cultural boundaries. In Scotland, these hybrid silver objects were new power symbols for emerging new kingdoms.[8]

Silver use changed once more with Viking contacts – yet also continued. Silver bullion was abundant again, and the range of uses expanded, still with a focus on jewellery, but now on arm-rings above all else. Yet brooches lived on, transformed in this contact – old local habits made new by Scandinavian styles, and becoming popular in contacts between older communities and these new arrivals, a sign of adaptation in a relationship often viewed through blood-tinted glasses. Silver was also still hacked. Viking Age hoards feature a new type of object that was designed from the outset to be chopped into pieces – worn around the wrist, ring-money was wealth worn on the body, simultaneously jewellery and bullion [11.5].

Fig. 11.5 (opposite): Intact and hacked Viking arm-rings from the Burray hoard; *c.*70mm (typical diameter), NMS X.IL 236–67 (selection).

SILVER IN CHANGING PLACES

Only parts of what is now Scotland had access to silver during the first millennium AD, and this varied over time. This wasn't due to underlying geology, constrained by where lead could be mined and silver extracted, because there is as yet no evidence of local silver extraction in our period. Instead, people depended on their contacts with silver-owning groups. Which areas had access to silver, and which did not? And what does this say about societies at the time?

Our first silver phase, the late 2nd-century Roman coinage, was limited in space as well as time [11.6a]. While occasional coins and hoards are found in far-flung parts, the real concentrations are in east–central Scotland, from the fringes of the Forth Valley to the Moray Firth. The second phase, based on Roman silver bullion from the late 3rd century onwards, was similar in outline though differing in detail.[9] Known hacksilver hoards, both Roman and Early Medieval, are an eastern Scottish phenomenon [11.6b]. So too are most of the massive silver chains [11.6c]. What can we glean by considering how and where silver was used in Scotland between the 2nd–6th centuries AD?

Some intriguing patterns emerge from this longer view of silver, including a curious gap in the spread of the coin hoards. None are known from East Lothian, though there was ample silver in the region later on – we know of the 23 kg Traprain Law Treasure buried in the early 5th century, and five massive silver chains found from the Lothians to the Lammermuirs. Other evidence tells us this had been an area friendly with the Roman Empire for centuries, and controlled by the rulers of Traprain Law who grew rich off Rome.[10] But it seems they didn't need to be bought off with quantities of *denarii* – they were already accustomed to a wide range of Roman objects, including silver coins, so these were no shiny novelty for them. Perhaps it was inappropriate to bribe such long-standing allies with silver in this way; existing ties already brought fine glass, pottery and metalwork to the hill.

By the 4th and 5th centuries AD, East Lothian's status as a firm and lasting ally of the Empire provided the quantities of silver required for the massive chains, and the cultural context which inspired development of this unique hybrid power symbol, spawned from interaction between local and late Roman military worlds. Might the chains have been a power symbol that distinguished this Roman ally from other (more fickle?) groups north of the frontier? While tight dating evidence remains elusive, scientific analysis of the chains suggests they could be earlier than usually thought – one from south-east Scotland appears to be made from undiluted late Roman silver [11.7], while their silver-alloy composition seems less variable than the (arguably) 5th-century hacksilver hoards of Norrie's Law and Gaulcross.[11] Does this reflect less recycling and an earlier deposition date? Were these new hybrid status symbols a 4th-century phenomenon created in this frontier world on the bounds of Empire?

The north-east of Scotland had a more chequered, boom-and-bust relationship with Rome. Roman coin payments had initially focused on Perth, Stirling and Fife, but attention shifted during the reign of the Emperor Severus (AD 193–211) to Aberdeenshire and Moray (and, to a lesser extent, Fife), perhaps to create a buffer zone around the most problematic areas. Intriguingly, these late

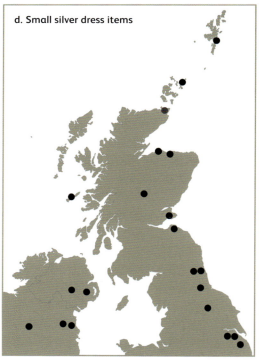

SCOTLAND'S EARLY SILVER

Fig. 11.6 a–d (opposite): Patterns in silver use in Scotland, c.AD 150–600: (a) Roman *denarius* hoards; (b) hacksilver hoards; (c) massive silver chains; (d) other non-Roman items.

Fig. 11.7 (left, above): Massive silver chain, Hoardweel, Scottish Borders; NMS IL.2009.15.5.

Fig. 11.8 (left, below): Pictish symbols on the massive silver chain clasp from Whitecleugh, South Lanarkshire; NMS X.FC 150.

2nd/early 3rd-century buffers are the same general areas in which we find later silver finds north of the Forth – the Dairsie Roman hacksilver hoard, northern silver chains and Early Medieval hacksilver hoards from Fife and Aberdeenshire, leap-frogging the area from the Tay to Stonehaven. It seems both local and Roman political relations persistently avoided this region.

The northern chains are so similar in morphology and technology to the southern ones that it seems most likely they were made in the south and moved north. This might have been through raiding, but the persistent pattern of silver connections makes them more likely to represent the exchange of objects as pledges (to guarantee verbal agreements) in alliances, personal links such as fostering, or payments to buy off northern tribes, echoing arrangements under the Roman world.

Two of the chains, both found beyond the core chain-using area of south-east Scotland, bear Pictish symbols [11.8] – what can they tell us? Like the chains, Pictish symbols probably developed through interaction between the late Roman military world and Iron Age tribes beyond the frontier. These seem to be a distinctively non-Roman form of literacy which was inspired by contact with the inscription-rich Roman world. New research suggests the earliest symbol usage belonged to the 3rd–4th centuries AD, and was more widespread and variable than that on the well-known later carved stones.[12] The symbols do not make the chains 'Pictish' (the meaning of such a term is very unclear at this time in any case), but both chains and symbols were part of these wider social developments on the edge of the late Roman world. Incised symbols on stones became widespread from Fife to the Northern and Western Isles, but the likely earliest examples are found on the coasts of the Moray Firth, Aberdeenshire and the Firth of Forth. There are fascinating hints of patterns to disentangle in this emerging story of the relationship between silver and symbols.[13]

The hacksilver hoards from Fife and Aberdeenshire, with their fragmented late Roman silver and clutch of rare objects, also pose fascinating questions. Why are they

CONCLUSION

143

Fig. 11.9: Crushed bowl rims, Norrie's Law hoard; NMS X.FC 89–90.

Fig. 11.10: Sites with evidence of silver-working in Scotland in the first millennium AD, divided broadly into pre- and post-AD 600, and those which cannot be closely dated.

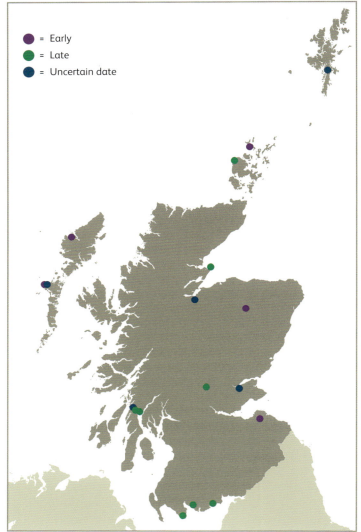

so similar when they lie 130 miles apart? Does this reflect shared material culture used in both areas, or access to a much wider reservoir of scrap silver? The rarity of such hoards makes this hard to assess, but there are clues. Some items were clearly part of a much wider world – the boss-rimmed bowl [11.9], and the possible helmet-fitting (page 89) both have continental parallels, while the mounts with incised decoration find British, Irish and near continental examples [7.29]. But all these are unknown in silver except in our Scottish hoards – an accident of survival, or reflection of local manufacture in a locally-available prestige material?

Some of the hoards' contents must have been local to Scotland.[14] The plaque with Pictish symbols from Fife is the most obvious example, but other potential candidates

SCOTLAND'S EARLY SILVER

144

include silver bangles. Found in both hoards, these evoke earlier power symbols in north-eastern Scotland, coiled massive bronze bracelets.[15] Other object types are found widely across Britain and Ireland in silver and bronze, such as handpins and spiral finger-rings, but their occurrence on Scottish settlement sites and the presence of manufacturing debris[16] indicates they were made and used here. This evidence also shows that silver was available (in relatively small quantities) and desirable in Scotland beyond the eastern focus of the coins, hacksilver and chains [11.10].[17]

By around AD 600, silver was more widespread, with traces of its re-melting now found in metal-working crucibles from sites across much of Scotland [11.10]. Some of these places were clearly high-status, perhaps even royal centres. In Atlantic-facing Scotland, silver was just one of several kinds of prestige item – powerful people here valued imported pottery, glass and exotic foodstuffs, other ways of making connections to a Mediterranean lifestyle.[18] Here, silver did not stand out like it did in the east of Scotland; people chose other ways to signal status. Sites like Dunadd in Argyll also show connections to the Anglo-Saxon world, with a willingness to use gold, new types of objects and new ways of decorating them. Now something extra was needed to mark out status and wider connections: gold, garnets, amber or other rare materials. Yet this is not the whole story. High-status sites have been fairly easy to find – forts and duns are easy to spot. But sites like Bruach an Druimein in Argyll and Cnoc a'Comhdhalach on North Uist show that silver was now being worked and brooches made on more humble settlements.[19]

SILVER BEYOND SCOTLAND

Our silver makes no sense unless we see it in a European view. Research in this area is still in its early stages,[20] but we see both links and differences to our Scottish story.

Our first phase, the *denarius* hoards, is a Scottish version of a European-scale phenomenon. From Ireland to the Caucasus there are hoards of Roman silver coins from the late 2nd century [3.3]. This was clearly a widespread Roman policy for the northern frontiers. But there were also marked differences. The distribution map shows gaps – some areas were avoided, or rejected this coinage. There were also big differences in how the coins were used. In Scotland, we argue for a dynamic and high-impact phenomenon: the coins were adopted, silver became all-important, and its withdrawal within the span of one or two generations served to undermine power-structures and caused dependent societies to crumble. *Denarii* are not found after the early 3rd century. This is very different from much of the continent, where these coins circulated through the 3rd and 4th centuries, while in areas such as central Germany there is clear evidence they were being cut up and melted for reuse.[21] The initial Roman policy may have been similar, but local responses to this were very varied.

This similar-and-different theme is also clear in the later Roman period, with hacksilver. Hoards with Roman hacksilver occur from Ireland to Ukraine [5.13]. While hacksilver was a Roman economic phenomenon, hoards dominated by it are very much a 'barbarian' habit, linked to diplomatic pay-offs or payment of soldiers. But there is a marked discrepancy between Britain and Ireland on one hand and the continent on the other; the islands have hoards purely of silver, whereas on the continent Roman gold played a key role too. This coloured what followed – gold was the power symbol of choice on the continent, though silver was far from forgotten. We have argued earlier that this related not only to availability (clearly much less gold reached beyond Hadrian's Wall, but it was not unknown) but also choice; silver was preferred in Scotland. Were there different cultural concepts of metals? Was silver valued because it was new, in contrast to gold which had a history here? Most of northern continental Europe had known no gold since the Bronze Age as there were no local sources, so gold and silver were equally exotic; given that the Romans valued gold over silver, societies may simply have adopted these external value systems. This was not the case in Scotland and Ireland; gold was available, but silver was preferred. Perhaps it conveyed an exoticness and a link to the power and legacy of Rome which gold did not; perhaps it emphasised difference to other areas. It shows that values were not absolute, but culturally conditioned.

After the end of the western Roman Empire, hoarding silver (and gold) continued in parts of the continent in a seemingly unbroken continuum. Hoards from Scandinavia, particularly Denmark, show how precious metal supplies were managed after the old Roman sources had dried up [11.11]. These hoards provide a good parallel for the Scottish silver from Norrie's Law and Gaulcross, with their late Roman fragments, a few Roman coins, and hacked versions of local jewellery.[22] But there are important differences too, including where they were buried. Denmark shows a clear link between silver caches and particular families, as many come from settlements; in Scotland, a repeated pattern of burial at ancient monuments suggests a different motivation behind their disposal, with silver separated from the world of the living.

Both links to the wider world and deliberate cultural differences are also clear in brooches – a key means of display. In what are now Scotland, Ireland and Wales, penannular brooches were the dominant type of the Early Medieval period. This was a marked contrast to England and much of the continent where a cross-shaped brooch derived from the late Roman crossbow form [5.22] and disc-shaped brooches (another late Roman form) were dominant. It seems likely that this was not happenstance but choice, to make a deliberate difference from neighbouring groups. And though the 7th and 8th centuries saw the creative artistic fusion that is Insular art, drawing on local influences from the islands, the Germanic world and the Mediterranean, some lines of demarcation hardened. The choice to wear a brooch bearing amber (used in Scotland and Ireland) or garnet (used in the Anglo-Saxon kingdoms) said a lot – crossover in this aspect was rare.[23] In Scotland, traditional brooch styles were retained, and the most prestigious objects were still made from silver underneath their thin veneers of gold.

The Viking Age brought new connections and new sources of silver, and new ideas of how to use it. Some of these connections are apparent in the coins from Viking Age hoards. Anglo-Saxon silver coins are found occasionally in Viking graves (where they are usually pierced for suspension) and abundantly in hoards, while Islamic silver *dirhams* occur in Viking Age hoards across Europe, including several hundred from Britain and Ireland. The practice of hacking and hoarding silver bullion also connects Scotland to other parts of the Viking world, while the

Fig. 11.11: Fragments from the hacksilver hoard from Mannerup, Denmark (buried around AD 500). On exhibition at Lejre Museum, Denmark. © Museum Organisation ROMU.

Fig. 11.12: Viking silver hoard from Burray, Orkney; NMS X.IL 236–67.

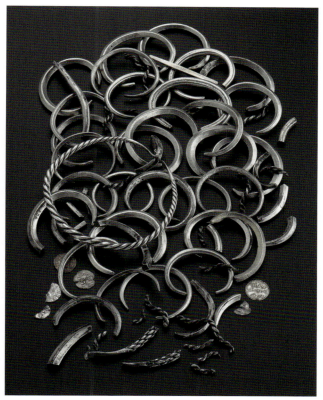

objects being hacked often show local influences – hybrid types of brooch and regional styles of arm-rings.

TREATING SILVER

Silver was valued – and as a result, it was rarely lost. While occasional small items might be accidentally dropped, most of the silver in museums today was deliberately buried, whether in a large hoard, a small cache, or as a single valued item such as the massive chains. These habits have a big impact on our evidence for Scotland's early silver. Precious objects could be handed down, hoarded or re-cycled, but were not committed to the grave, in contrast to areas such as the early Anglo-Saxon world. Do isolated finds of jewellery represent separate burials after a person's death, perhaps because they were too personal to remain in view? Could this explain the solitary chains? Or was all this silver buried for safekeeping? This commonsense approach to wealth superficially appeals to our money-driven minds – in the absence of banks, is this the ancient equivalent of hiding cash under the mattress? It's likely that some hoards were indeed buried to keep them safe, and never recovered. Indeed, this is the dominant interpretation of Viking Age hoards – stashes of wealth, buried at troubled times [11.12]. Yet contemporary Norse sources give a very different view of such hoards – for the wealth you buried in life, placing it under the protection of the gods, would be retrieved in the afterlife. At this most unsettled of times, it seems that religion, not pragmatism, governed the burial of many hoards.

This idea of religious or social motives behind the burial of wealth rather than purely practical ones has repeated confirmation from the findspots. Silver was

CONCLUSION

buried in places where it would be, to say the least, tricky to recover – river margins, peat bogs, waterlogged caves. To this we may add ancient monuments, for a surprising number of our Scottish silver finds come from older ritual sites. Surely these were more than just memorable places in the landscape – you don't need to be a Tolkien fiend to appreciate the power of ancient monuments in a superstitious society, where the ghosts of ancestors and shadows of gods might lurk in every old stone.

CONCLUSIONS: A LONG VIEW OF SILVER

Today, silver is everyday; silver brooches, ear-rings or pendants are nothing out of the ordinary. It has lost much of its power to impress, though on the rare occasions we see a table laid with gleaming silver dishes it still looks special. We see gold as the 'gold standard' of value. Yet this was not the case in Scotland a thousand years ago. Silver, not gold, was the real mark of value. It was rare and exotic with a striking sheen, marking links to Roman favour or legacy, and connections to a wider world.

Our story is a tale of the unexpected. We have looked at a time when coins were useless for spending but still had value, for showing off. We have looked at a period when silver was better than gold, it seems. And we have looked at times when wealth was buried not for safekeeping but as a sacrifice. Silver was not hoarded to keep it safe, but given away to win the favour of gods or the prestige of your peers. It is hard for us to recalibrate our views – but we need to. Because, for a thousand years, silver was the most powerful material in Scotland.

NOTES

1. See chapter 1.
2. See chapters 2 and 3.
3. See chapters 4 and 5.
4. See chapter 6.
5. See chapter 8.
6. See chapter 7.
7. See chapter 9.
8. The finds from Dunadd in Argyll, which became the centre of the kingdom of Dál Riata, are a good example. Ewan Campbell has argued that Dunadd achieved its key role when separate kin-groups in the area came together in the 7th century. The rulers of this new amalgamated kingdom cemented their position by acting as a central exchange point and craft centre, drawing on wide influences to create precious-metal artefacts which marked an individual's position and were used in gift exchange (Campbell 2009). At a larger scale, brooches were used as badges of cultural affiliations from the 8th century – the main styles of brooches used in Scotland are different from those used in Ireland (Goldberg 2015b, 196).
9. The overlap with areas which previously received coins is partial, suggesting that these different silver distributions reflect a longer-running Roman diplomatic concern with the eastern seaboard rather than long-term policy driven to particular favoured groups.
10. Jobey 1976; Hunter 2009b.
11. Observations we have drawn from a long-running analytical programme in National Museums Scotland laboratories as part of the Glenmorangie Research Project by Dr Lore Troalen and Dr Susy Kirk; it is intended to consider these tricky questions more fully in a separate publication.
12. Noble, Goldberg and Hamilton in preparation.
13. Clarke, Blackwell and Goldberg 2012, 169; Goldberg in preparation.
14. Though we cannot fix their production spot with any real precision.
15. Of 1st / 2nd-century date; MacGregor 1976, nos 213–9.
16. Indeed, mould evidence shows that handpins were made in Atlantic Scotland: Heald 2001; McDonnell and Milns 2015, 411–3.
17. Dating many of the sites with evidence of silver-working is tricky, as most are old finds; Fig. 11.10 attempts to divide them into pre- and post-AD 600, but this is not always possible.
18. Campbell 2007.
19. Campbell and Heald 2007, 176.
20. What follows is informed by initial results from an AHRC Research Network 'Silver, Status and Society: transition from late Roman to Early Medieval Europe'. We are grateful to the participants in this network for their insights and enthusiasm.
21. Voß 2013, 310, table 2; Rau 2013a, 353.
22. Dyhrfjeld-Johnsen 2013; Rau 2013b.
23. An observation by one of us (AB) in the course of research into Early Medieval metalwork; only the Ripon jewel used both amber and garnet, to our knowledge.

Bibliography

ANCIENT SOURCES

Dio Cassius. *Roman history* (translations from Ireland 2008).

Herodian. *History of the Roman Empire since Marcus Aurelius* (translations from Ireland 2008).

REFERENCES

Abdy, R 2013. 'The Patching hoard', in Hunter and Painter (eds) 2013a, 107–15.

Alexander, J J G 1976. 'The illustrated manuscripts of the Notitia Dignitatum', in R Goodburn and P Bartholomew (eds), *Aspects of the Notitia Dignitatum*, 11–49. Oxford: BAR (BAR Supplementary Series 15).

Allason-Jones, L 2014. 'Zoomorphic brooches: decoration or religious ideology?', in S-R Marzel and G D Stiebel (eds), *Dress and ideology: fashioning identity from Antiquity to the present*, 69–87. London: Bloomsbury.

Allen, M 2011. 'Silver production and the money supply in England and Wales, 1086–1500', *Economic History Review* 64, 114–31.

Alston, R 1994. 'Roman military pay from Caesar to Diocletian', *Journal of Roman Studies* 84, 113–23.

Anon 1888. 'Donations to the Museum', *Proceedings of the Society of Antiquaries of Scotland* 22 (1887–8), 268.

Baratte, F and Painter, K (eds) 1989. *Trésors d'orfèvrerie gallo-romains*. Paris: Éditions de la Réunion des musées nationaux.

Barnes, M P and Page, R I 2006. *The runic inscriptions of Britain*. Uppsala: Institutionen för nordiska språk vid Uppsala universitet.

Baron, S, Tamas, C and Le Carlier, C 2014. 'How mineralogy and geochemistry can improve the significance of Pb isotopes in metal provenance studies', *Archaeometry* 56 (4), 665–80.

Barrett, J H 2007. 'The pirate fishermen: the political economy of a Medieval maritime society', in B B Smith, S Taylor and G Williams (eds), *West over Sea: studies in Scandinavian sea-borne expansion and settlement before 1300*, 299–340. Leiden: Brill.

Barrett, J H 2008. 'What caused the Viking age?', *Antiquity* 82 (317), 671–85.

Barrow, G W S 1973. *The Kingdom of the Scots*. London: Edward Arnold.

Bateson, J D and Hanson, W S 1990. 'A Flavian hoard from Scotland: a foundation deposit ?', *Numismatic Chronicle* 150, 233–6.

Bateson, J D 2007. 'Coins', in Hanson 2007a, 253–70.

Bayley, J 2009. 'The discovery of precious metal refining in Roman Chichester', in J-F Moreau (ed), *Proceedings of the 36th international symposium on archaeometry*, 425–32. Quebec: CELAT.

Bayley, J, Dungworth, D and Paynter, S 2001. *Centre for Archaeology guidelines: archaeometallurgy*. Available at: https://historicengland.org.uk/images-books/publications/archaeometallurgy-guidelines-best-practice/ [accessed 3/8/2017]

Bayley, J and Eckstein, K 1998. *Metalworking debris from Pentrehyling Fort, Brompton, Shropshire*. Swindon: English Heritage (Ancient Monuments Laboratory Report 13/98).

Beck, L, Bosonnet, S, Réveillon, S, Eliot, D and Pilon, F 2004. 'Silver surface enrichment of silver-copper alloys: a limitation for the analysis of ancient silver coins by surface techniques', *Nuclear Instruments and Methods in Physics Research B* 226 (1–2), 153–62.

Bennett, A 1994. 'Technical examination and conservation', in M M Mango and A Bennett, *The Sevso treasure: part one*, 21–35. Ann Arbor: Journal of Roman Archaeology (Supplementary Series 12).

Benton, S 1931. 'The excavation of the Sculptor's Cave, Covesea, Morayshire', *Proceedings of the Society of Antiquaries of Scotland* 65 (1930–1), 177–216.

Birley, A R 2005. *The Roman government of Britain*. Oxford: Oxford University Press.

Birley, E 1955. Review of Grünhagen 1954, *Antiquity* 29, 246.

Black, G F 1895. 'Descriptive catalogue of antiquities found in Ayrshire and Wigtownshire and now in the National Museum, Edinburgh', *Archaeological Collections of Ayrshire and Galloway* 7, 1–47.

Blackburn, M A S and Pagan, H E 1986. 'A revised check-list of coin hoards from the British Isles, *c*.500–1100', in M A S Blackburn (ed), *Anglo-Saxon monetary history: essays in memory of Michael Dolley*, 291–313. Leicester: Leicester University Press.

Blackwell, A and Goldberg, M forthcoming. 'Norrie's Law, Gaulcross and beyond: widening the context of hacksilver hoarding in Scotland', in A Blackwell (ed), *Scotland in Early Medieval Europe*. Leiden: Sidestone Press.

Bland, R 1997. 'The changing patterns of hoards of precious-metal coins in the late Empire', *Antiquité Tardive* 5, 29–55.

Bland, R 2012. 'Gold for the barbarians? Uniface gold medallions of the House of Constantine found in Britain and Ireland', *Britannia* 43, 217–25.

Bland, R and Loriot, X 2010. *Roman and early Byzantine gold coins found in Britain and Ireland*. London: Royal Numismatic Society.

Bland, R, Moorhead, S and Walton, P 2013. 'Finds of late Roman silver coins from Britain: the contribution of the Portable Antiquities Scheme', in Hunter and Painter (eds) 2013a, 117–66.

Böhme, H W 2000. 'The Vermand treasure', in K Reynolds Brown, D Kidd and C T Little (eds), *From Attila to Charlemagne: arts of the Early Medieval period in the Metropolitan Museum of Art*, 78–89. New York: Metropolitan Museum of Art.

Booth, A 2015. *Reassessing the long chronology of the penannular brooch in Britain: exploring changing styles, use and meaning across a millennium*. Unpublished PhD thesis, University of Leicester.

Bradley, R 1987. 'Time regained: the creation of continuity', *Journal of the British Archaeological Association* 140, 1–17.

Bradley, R, Clarke, A and Hunter, F 2016. 'Excavations at Waulkmill, Tarland, Aberdeenshire: a Neolithic pit, Roman Iron Age burials and an earlier prehistoric stone circle', in R Bradley and C Nimura (eds), *The use and reuse of stone circles. Fieldwork at five Scottish monuments and its implications*, 27–55. Oxford: Oxbow.

Bradley, R and Williams, H (eds) 1998. *The past in the past: the reuse of ancient monuments* (= *World Archaeology* 30: 1). London: Routledge.

Braund, D 1984. *Rome and the friendly king: the character of the client kingship*. London: Croom Helm.

Breeze, A 1998. 'Pictish chains and Welsh forgeries', *Proceedings of the Society of Antiquaries of Scotland* 128, 481–4.

Breeze, D J 1982. *The northern frontiers of Roman Britain*. London: Batsford.

Bruce-Mitford, R 2005. *A corpus of late Celtic hanging-bowls*. Oxford: Oxford University Press.

Buist, G 1839. *The silver armour of Norrie's Law*. Cupar: Fifeshire Journal Office.

Burley, E 1956. 'A catalogue and survey of the metal-work from Traprain Law', *Proceedings of the Society of Antiquaries of Scotland* 89 (1955–6), 118–226.

Burnett, C and Tabraham, C 1993. *The Honours of Scotland. The story of the Scottish crown jewels*. Edinburgh: Historic Scotland.

Bursche, A 1999. 'Die Rolle römischer Goldmedallione in der Spätantike', in Seipel (ed) 1999, 39–53.

Bursche, A 2000. 'Roman gold medallions in Barbaricum. Symbols of power and prestige of Germanic élite in Late Antiquity', in B Kluge and B Weisser (eds), *XII. Internationaler Numismatischer Kongress, Berlin 1997. Akten – Proceedings – Actes*, 758–71. Berlin: Staatlichen Museen zu Berlin – Preußischer Kulturbesitz.

Bursche, A 2001. 'Roman gold medallions as power symbols of the Germanic élite', in Magnus (ed) 2001, 84–102.

Butcher, K and Ponting, M 2012. 'The beginning of the end? The denarius in the second century', *Numismatic Chronicle* 172, 63–83.

Butcher, K and Ponting, M 2014. *The metallurgy of Roman silver coinage from the reform of Nero to the reform of Trajan*. Oxford: Oxford University Press.

Cahn, H and Kaufmann-Heinimann, A 1984. *Der spätrömische Silberschatz von Kaiseraugst*. Derendingen: Habegger Verlag.

Campbell, B 1994. *The Roman army 31 BC–AD 337. A sourcebook*. London: Routledge.

Campbell, E 2007. *Continental and Mediterranean imports to Atlantic Britain and Ireland, AD 400–800*. York: Council for British Archaeology (CBA Research Report 157).

Campbell, E 2009. 'Anglo-Saxon/Gaelic interaction in Scotland', in J Graham-Campbell and M Ryan (eds), *Anglo-Saxon/Irish relations before the Vikings*, 253–63. Oxford: Oxford University Press for The British Academy.

Campbell, E and Heald, A 2007. 'A Pictish brooch mould from North Uist: implications for the organisation of non-ferrous metalworking in the later 1st millennium AD', *Medieval Archaeology* 51, 172–8.

Campbell, E, Driscoll, S, Gondek, M and Maldonado, A forthcoming. 'An early medieval and prehistoric nexus: the Strathearn Environs and Royal Forteviot project', in A Blackwell (ed), *Scotland in Early Medieval Europe*. Leiden: Sidestone Press.

Carson, R A G and O'Kelly, C 1977. 'A catalogue of the Roman coins from Newgrange, Co. Meath, and notes on the coins and related finds', *Proceedings of the Royal Irish Academy* 77C, 35–55.

Casey, P J 1980. *Roman coinage in Britain*. Princes Risborough: Shire.

Cessford, C 1997. 'The crossbow brooch from Carn Liath', *Pictish Arts Society Journal* 11, 19–22.

Charlesworth, D 1973. 'The Aesica hoard', *Archaeologia Aeliana* (5th series) 1, 225–34.

Clark, N D L 2014. *Scottish gold: fruit of the nation*. Glasgow: The Hunterian, University of Glasgow.

Clarke, D 2008. *St Ninian's Isle treasure*. Edinburgh: NMS Enterprises Ltd – Publishing.

Clarke, D V, Blackwell, A and Goldberg, M 2012. *Early Medieval Scotland: individuals, communities and ideas*. Edinburgh: NMS Enterprises Ltd – Publishing.

Clarke, D V and Heald, A 2008. 'A new date for "Pictish" symbols', *Medieval Archaeology* 52, 291–310.

Claughton, P 2003. 'Production and economic impact: northern Pennine (English) silver in the 12th century', *Proceedings of the 6th international mining history congress, September 26–29, 2003, Akabira City, Hokkaido, Japan*, 146–9. Akabira City: Taiyo Hokkaido Community Support Foundation.

Close-Brooks, J 1986. 'Excavations at Clatchard Craig, Fife', *Proceedings of the Society of Antiquaries of Scotland* 116, 117–84.

Cochran-Patrick, R 1876. *Records of the coinage of Scotland*. Edinburgh: Edmonston and Douglas.

Coles, F R 1906. 'Report on stone circles surveyed in the North-East of Scotland, chiefly in Banffshire, with measured plans and drawings, obtained under the Gunning Fellowship', *Proceedings of the Society of Antiquaries of Scotland* 40, 164–206.

Collingwood, R G and Wright, R P (S S Frere and R S O Tomlin, eds) 1991a. *The Roman inscriptions of Britain volume II: instrumentum domesticum. Fascicule 1*. Stroud: Alan Sutton.

Collingwood, R G and Wright, R P (S S Frere and R S O Tomlin, eds) 1991b. *The Roman inscriptions of Britain volume II: instrumentum domesticum. Fascicule 2*. Stroud: Alan Sutton.

Collingwood, R G and Wright, R P (S S Frere and R S O Tomlin, eds) 1991c. *The Roman inscriptions of Britain volume II: instrumentum domesticum. Fascicule 3*. Stroud: Alan Sutton.

Collins, R 2010. 'Brooch use in the 4th- to 5th-century frontier', in Collins and Allason-Jones (eds) 2010, 64–77.

Collins, R and Allason-Jones, L (eds) 2010. *Finds from the frontier: material culture in the 4th–5th centuries*. York: Council for British Archaeology (CBA Research Report 162).

Cool, H E M 2000. 'The significance of snake jewellery hoards', *Britannia* 31, 29–40.

Cool, H E M 2006. *Eating and drinking in Roman Britain*. Cambridge: Cambridge University Press.

Cottam, E, de Jersey, P, Rudd, C and Sills, J 2010. *Ancient British coins*. Aylsham: Chris Rudd.

Creighton, J 2000. *Coins and power in late Iron Age Britain*. Cambridge: Cambridge University Press.

Creighton, J 2014. 'The supply and movement of *denarii* in Roman Britain', *Britannia* 45, 121–63.

Critch, A 2015. *How are princely gifts repaid by your powerful friends?' Ring-money and the appropriation of tradition in Insular Viking politics, AD 900–1065*. Unpublished PhD thesis, University of Cambridge.

Curle, A O 1923. *The Treasure of Traprain: a Scottish hoard of Roman silver plate*. Glasgow: Maclehose.

Curle, A O n.d. *The journal of A O Curle – 1913 to 1954*. Typed manuscript, Historic Environment Scotland Search Room (H2 CUR).

Curle, C L 1982. *Pictish and Norse finds from the Brough of Birsay*. Edinburgh: Society of Antiquaries of Scotland.

Curle, J 1932. 'An inventory of objects of Roman and provincial Roman origin found on sites in Scotland not definitely associated with Roman constructions', *Proceedings of the Society of Antiquaries of Scotland* 66 (1931–2), 277–397.

Dembski, G 2005. *Die antiken Gemmen und Kameen aus Carnuntum*. Vienna: Phoibos Verlag.

Dennis, M 2008. 'Silver of the Iceni', *Current Archaeology* 217, 20–3.

Dockrill, S, Bond, J, Turner, V, Brown, L, Bashford, D, Cussans, J and

Nicholson, R 2015. *Excavations at Old Scatness, Shetland, volume 2: the broch and Iron Age village*. Lerwick: Shetland Heritage Publications.

Doračić, D, Lang, J and Fletcher P 2015. 'Late Roman silver hoard from Vinkovci, Croatia – a preliminary technological overview', *Historical Metallurgy* 49 (2), 87–95.

Driscoll, S T 1998. 'Picts and prehistory: cultural resource management in early medieval Scotland', in Bradley and Williams (eds) 1998, 142–58.

Dyhrfjeld-Johnsen, M 2013. 'Danish Hacksilber hoards: a status report', in Hunter and Painter (eds) 2013a, 321–38.

Ellis, L (ed) 2000. *Archaeological theory and method: an encyclopedia*. New York: Taylor and Francis.

Erdrich, M 2002. *Corpus der römischen Funde im europäischen Barbaricum. Deutschland Band 4*. Bonn: Habelt.

Etchingham, C and Swift, C 2004 'English and Pictish terms for brooch in an 8th-century Irish law-text', *Medieval Archaeology* 48, 31–49.

Evans, E 2000. *The Caerleon canabae: excavations in the civil settlement 1984–1990*. London: Society for the Promotion of Roman Studies (Britannia Monograph 16).

Fairburn, R A 2007. 'A tenth century lead smelting site in West Allendale', *British Mining* 83, 47–51.

Farley, J and Hunter, F (eds) 2015. *Celts: art and identity*. London: British Museum/Edinburgh: NMS Enterprises Ltd – Publishing.

Ferguson, R B and Whitehead, N L 1999. *War in the tribal zone: expanding states and indigenous warfare* (2nd edition). Santa Fe: School of American Research Press.

Forsyth, K 1995. 'Language in Pictland: spoken and written', in E H Nicoll and K Forsyth (eds), *A Pictish panorama: the story of the Picts*, 7–10. Brechin: Pinkfoot Press.

Forsyth, K 2005. 'Hic memoria perpetua: the early inscribed stones of southern Scotland in context', in S Foster and M Cross (eds), *Able minds and practised hands: Scotland's early medieval sculpture in the 21st century*, 113–34: Society for Medieval Archaeology (Monograph 23).

Fowler, E 1960. 'The origins and development of the penannular brooch in Europe', *Proceedings of the Prehistoric Society* 26, 149–77.

Fowler, E 1963. 'Celtic metalwork of the fifth and sixth centuries A.D.: a re-appraisal', *Archaeological Journal* 120, 98–160.

Fraser, I 2008. *The Pictish symbol stones of Scotland*. Edinburgh: Royal Commission on the Ancient and Historical Monuments of Scotland.

Fraser, J E 2005. *The Roman conquest of Caledonia: the battle of Mons Graupius AD 84*. Stroud: Tempus.

Fraser, J E 2009. *From Caledonia to Pictland: Scotland to 795*. Edinburgh: Edinburgh University Press.

Gardiner, V 2001. 'An analysis of Romano-British lead pigs', *Institute for Archaeo-Metallurgical Studies Newsletter* 21, 11–13.

Gavin, F 2013. 'Insular Military-Style silver pins in late Iron Age Ireland', in Hunter and Painter (eds), 2013a, 427–39.

Gavin, F and Newman, C 2007. 'Notes on Insular silver in the "Military Style"', *Journal of Irish Archaeology* 16, 1–10.

Gerrard, J 2013. *The ruin of Roman Britain: an archaeological perspective*. Cambridge: Cambridge University Press.

Gitler, H and Ponting, M 2003. *The silver coinage of Septimius Severus and his family (193–211 AD): a study of the chemical composition of the Roman and eastern issues*. Milan: Edizioni ennerre.

Goldberg, M 2015a. 'Out of a Roman world, *c*. AD 250–650', in Farley and Hunter (eds) 2015, 152–71.

Goldberg, M 2015b. 'At the western edge of the Christian world, c. AD 600–900', in Farley and Hunter (eds) 2015, 172–205.

Goldberg, M in preparation. 'Conventions in carving: a relative chronology for the Pictish symbol system'.

Goldberg, M and Blackwell, A 2013. 'The different histories of the Norrie's Law hoard', in Hawkes (ed) 2013, 326–38.

Goldsworthy, A 2009. *The fall of the West: the death of the Roman superpower*. London: Weidenfield and Nicholson.

Graham, A 1956. 'A memorial of Alexander Ormiston Curle', *Proceedings of the Society of Antiquaries of Scotland* 88 (1954–6), 234–6.

Graham-Campbell, J 1985. 'A lost Pictish treasure (and two Viking-age gold arm-rings) from the Broch of Burgar, Orkney', *Proceedings of the Society of Antiquaries of Scotland* 115, 241–61.

Graham-Campbell, J 1991. 'Norrie's Law, Fife: on the nature and dating of the silver hoard', *Proceedings of the Society of Antiquaries of Scotland* 121, 241–59.

Graham-Campbell, J 1995. *The Viking-Age gold and silver of Scotland*. Edinburgh: National Museums Scotland.

Graham-Campbell, J 2013. *The Cuerdale hoard and related Viking-Age silver and gold from Britain and Ireland in the British Museum* (2nd amended printing). London: British Museum.

Graham-Campbell, J and Batey, C E 1998. *Vikings in Scotland: an archaeological survey*. Edinburgh: Edinburgh University Press.

Graham-Campbell, J and Williams, G (eds) 2007. *Silver economy in the Viking Age*. Walnut Creek, CA: Left Coast Press.

Grane, T 2013. 'Roman relations with southern Scandinavia in Late Antiquity', in Hunter and Painter (eds) 2013a, 359–71.

Grønlund Evers, K 2011. *The Vindolanda tablets and the ancient economy*. Oxford: Archaeopress (BAR British Series 544).

Grünhagen, W 1954. *Der Schatzfund von Gross Bodungen*. Berlin: de Gruyter / Römisch-Germanische Kommission (Römisch-Germanische Forschungen 21).

Guest, P 2008. 'Roman gold and Hun kings: the use and hoarding of solidi in the late fourth and fifth centuries', in A Bursche, R Ciołek and R Wolters (eds), *Roman coins outside the Empire: ways and phases, contexts and functions*, 295–307. Wetteren: Moneta.

Guest, P 2013. 'Siliquae from the Traprain Law treasure: silver and society in later fourth- and fifth-century Britain', in Hunter and Painter (eds) 2013a, 93–106.

Guggisberg, M A 2013. 'Silver and donatives: non-coin exchange within and outside the Roman empire', in Hunter and Painter (eds) 2013a, 193–212.

Guggisberg, M and Kaufmann-Heinimann, A 2003. *Der spätrömische Silberschatz von Kaiseraugst. Die neuen Funde*. Augst: Römerstadt Augusta Raurica.

Guiraud, H 1989. 'Bagues et anneaux à l'époque romaine en Gaule', *Gallia* 46, 173–211.

Hamilton, J R C 1968. *Excavations at Clickhimin, Shetland*. Edinburgh: HMSO.

Hanson, W S 2007a. *Elginhaugh: a Flavian fort and its annexe*. London: Roman Society.

Hanson, W S 2007b. *Elginhaugh: a Roman frontier fort in Scotland*. Stroud: Tempus.

Hanson, W and Maxwell, G 1986. *The Antonine Wall: Rome's north-west frontier* (2nd edition). Edinburgh: Edinburgh University Press.

Hardt, M 2015. 'Childerich I. in den historischen Quellen', in Quast (ed) 2015a, 217–24.

Harhoiu, R 1977. *The fifth-century AD treasure from Pietroasa, Romania, in the light of recent research*. Oxford: BAR (BAR Supplementary Series 24).

Harvey, W S 1997. 'Lead mining in medieval Scotland', *British Mining: Memoirs of the Northern Mine Research Society* 59, 123–7.

Hawkes, J (ed) 2013. *Making histories: proceedings of the sixth international conference of Insular art, York 2011*. Donington: Shaun Tyas.

Heald, A 2001. 'Knobbed spearbutts of the British and Irish Iron Age: new examples and new thoughts', *Antiquity* 75, 689–96.

Heald, A 2005. *Non-ferrous metalworking in Iron Age Scotland 700 BC–AD 700*. Unpublished PhD dissertation, University of Edinburgh.

Heather, P 2007. *The fall of the Roman Empire: a new history*. London: Pan.

Heather, P 2017. 'The late Roman imperial centre and its northwest frontier', in Roymans, Heeren and De Clercq (eds) 2017, 11–38.

Hedges, J 1987. *Bu, Gurness and the brochs of Orkney. Part II: Gurness*. Oxford: BAR (BAR British Series 164).

Henderson, I 1967. *The Picts*. London: Thames and Hudson.

Henig, M 2007. *A corpus of Roman engraved gemstones from British sites* (3rd edition). Oxford: Archaeopress (BAR British Series 8).

Hobbs, R 2006. *Late Roman precious metal deposits c. AD 200–700: changes over time and space*. Oxford: Archaeopress (BAR International Series 1504).

Hobbs, R 2016. *The Mildenhall treasure: late Roman silver plate from East Anglia*. London: British Museum.

Hodgson, N 2009. 'Elginhaugh: the most complete fort plan in the Roman empire', *Britannia* 40, 365–8.

Hodgson, N 2014. 'The British expedition of Septimius Severus', *Britannia* 45, 31–51.

Holmes, N M McQ 2006. 'Two denarius hoards from Birnie, Moray', *British Numismatic Journal* 76, 1–44.

Holmes, N M McQ 2012. 'The Roman coins from Newstead in context', in F Hunter and L Keppie (eds), *A Roman frontier post and its people: Newstead 1911–2011*, 123–35. Edinburgh: NMS Enterprises Ltd – Publishing.

Holmes, N M McQ 2014. 'The Synton and Kippilaw denarius hoards: further numismatic evidence for late Antonine and Severan Scotland', *Proceedings of the Society of Antiquaries of Scotland* 144, 133–67.

Holmes, N and Hunter, F 2001. 'Roman counterfeiters' moulds from Scotland', *Proceedings of the Society of Antiquaries of Scotland* 131, 167–76.

Hook, D and Callewaert, M 2013. 'Appendix 2: The scientific examination and analysis of some of the Roman silver artefacts from the Coleraine Treasure', in Marzinzik 2013, 184–6.

Hope-Taylor, B 1977. *Yeavering, an Anglo-British centre of early Northumbria*. London: HMSO.

Horsnæs, H 2010. *Crossing boundaries. An analysis of Roman coins in Danish contexts. Vol 1: finds from Sealand, Funen and Jutland*. Copenhagen: National Museum.

Houston, A McN 1924. *Auchterderran (Fife): a parish history*. Paisley: Alexander Gardner.

Hughes, M, Lang, J, La Niece, S and Oddy, A 1989. 'Technologie de l'argenterie romaine', in Baratte and Painter (eds) 1989, 21–8.

Hunter, F 1997. 'Iron Age coins in Scotland', *Proceedings of the Society of Antiquaries of Scotland* 127, 513–25.

Hunter, F 2006. 'Recent finds from Strageath Roman fort', *Tayside and Fife Archaeological Journal* 12, 81–8.

Hunter, F 2007a. 'Silver for the barbarians: interpreting denarii hoards in north Britain and beyond', in R Hingley and S Willis (eds), *Roman finds: context and theory*, 214–24. Oxford: Oxbow.

Hunter, F 2007b. *Beyond the edge of the Empire: Caledonians, Picts and Romans*. Rosemarkie: Groam House Museum.

Hunter, F 2007c. 'Lead beads', in R Toolis, 'Intermittent occupation and forced abandonment: excavation of an Iron Age promontory fort at Carghidown, Dumfries and Galloway', *Proceedings of the Society of Antiquaries of Scotland* 137, 265–318 (282–9).

Hunter, F 2009a. 'Recent work on "stray finds" of Roman objects in East Lothian', in C Haselgrove, *The Traprain Law Environs Project. Fieldwork and excavations 2000–2004*, 259–65. Edinburgh: Society of Antiquaries of Scotland.

Hunter, F 2009b. 'Traprain Law and the Roman world', in W S Hanson (ed), *The army and frontiers of Rome*, 225–40. Portsmouth, Rhode Island: Journal of Roman Archaeology (Supplementary Series).

Hunter, F 2009c. 'Miniature masterpieces: unusual Iron Age brooches from Scotland', in G Cooney, K Becker, J Coles, M Ryan and S Sievers (eds), *Relics of old decency: archaeological studies in later prehistory. A Festschrift for Barry Raftery*, 143–55. Dublin: Wordwell.

Hunter, F 2010. 'Beyond the frontier: interpreting late Roman Iron Age indigenous and imported material culture', in Collins and Allason-Jones (eds) 2010, 96–109.

Hunter, F 2014a. 'Art in context: the massive metalworking tradition of north-east Scotland', in C Gosden, S Crawford and K Ulmschneider (eds), *Celtic art in Europe: making connections. Essays in honour of Vincent Megaw on his 80th birthday*, 325–40. Oxford: Oxbow.

Hunter, F 2014b. 'Looking over the Wall: the Late and Post-Roman Iron Age north of Hadrian's Wall', in F K Haarer (ed), *AD 410: the history and archaeology of late and post-Roman Britain*, 206–15. London: Roman Society.

Hunter, F 2015. 'The lure of silver: denarius hoards and relations across the frontier', in D J Breeze, R H Jones and I A Oltean (eds), *Understanding Roman frontiers*, 251–69. Edinburgh: Birlinn.

Hunter, F forthcoming a. 'The non-ferrous finds', in I Armit and L Büster, *Excavations at Sculptor's Cave, Covesea, Moray*. Edinburgh: Society of Antiquaries of Scotland.

Hunter, F forthcoming b. 'The copper-alloy finds', in S Birch, G Cruickshanks and J McKenzie, *High Pasture Cave: ritual, memory and identity in Iron Age Skye*. Oxford: Oxbow

Hunter, F and Davis, M 1994. 'Early Bronze Age lead – a unique necklace from southeast Scotland', *Antiquity* 68, 824–30.

Hunter, F and Davis, M 2000. 'Necklace', in F Hunter, 'Excavation of an Early Bronze Age cemetery and other sites at West Water Reservoir, West Linton, Scottish Borders', *Proceedings of the Society of Antiquaries of Scotland* 130, 115–82 (136–41).

Hunter, F and Painter, K (eds) 2013a. *Late Roman silver: the Traprain Treasure in context*. Edinburgh: Society of Antiquaries of Scotland.

Hunter, F and Painter, K 2013b. 'Preface', in Hunter and Painter (eds) 2013a, xvii–xxiv.

Hunter, F and Painter, K 2017. 'Hacksilber in the Late Roman and Early Medieval world – economics, frontier politics and imperial legacies', in Roymans, Heeren and De Clercq (eds) 2017, 81–96.

Idoine, N E, Bide, T, Brown, T J, and Raycraft, E R 2016. *United Kingdom minerals yearbook 2015*. Nottingham: British Geological Survey.

Ingemark, D 2014. *Glass, alcohol and power in Roman Iron Age Scotland*. Edinburgh: NMS Enterprises Ltd – Publishing.

Ireland, S 2008. *Roman Britain: a sourcebook* (3rd edition). London: Routledge.

Janiszewski, R 2011. 'A fragment of a gold bracelet from Newgrange, Co. Meath, and its late Roman context', *Journal of Irish Archaeology* 20, 53–63.

Janiszewski, R 2012. 'A late Roman object from Cove, Dumfries and Galloway, rediscovered', *Proceedings of the Society of Antiquaries of Scotland* 142, 133–44.

Jobey, G 1976. 'Traprain Law: a summary', in D W Harding (ed), *Hillforts: later prehistoric earthworks in Britain and Ireland*, 191–204. London: Academic Press.

Johns, C 1974. 'A Roman silver pin from Oldcroft, Gloucestershire', *Antiquaries Journal* 54, 295–7.

Johns, C 1996a. 'Hacked, broken or chopped? A matter of terminology', *Antiquaries Journal* 76, 228–30.

Johns, C 1996b. *The jewellery of Roman Britain: Celtic and classical traditions*. London: UCL Press.

Johns, C and Potter, T 1983. *The Thetford treasure: Roman jewellery and silver*. London: British Museum.

Jones, A H M 1964. *The later Roman empire 284–602: a social, economic and administrative survey*. Oxford: Basil Blackwell.

Jørgensen, L and Vang Petersen, P 1998. *Gold, power and belief. Danish gold treasures from prehistory and the Middle Ages*. Copenhagen: Nationalmuseet / Thaning and Appel.

Kassiandou, V 2003. 'Early extraction of silver from complex polymetallic ores', in P Craddock and J Lang (eds), *Mining and metal production through the ages*, 198–206. London: British Museum.

Kaufmann-Heinimann, A 2013. 'The Traprain treasure: survey and perspectives', in Hunter and Painter (eds) 2013a, 243–61.

Kaufmann-Heinimann, A and Martin, M 2017. *Die Apostelkanne und das Tafelsilber im Hortfund von 1628: Trierer Silberschätze des 5. Jarhunderts*. Trier: Rheinisches Landesmuseum Trier

Kelly, E 2001. 'The Hillquarter, Co Westmeath mounts: an early medieval saddle from Ireland', in M Redknap, N Edwards, S Youngs, A Lane and J Knight (eds), *Pattern and purpose in Insular art. Proceedings of the fourth international conference on Insular art held at the National Museum and Gallery, Cardiff 3–6 September 1998*, 261–74. Oxford: Oxbow.

Kelly, F 2005. *A guide to early Irish law* (reprint of 1988 edition). Dublin: School of Celtic Studies, Dublin Institute for Advanced Studies.

Künzl, E (ed) 1993. *Die Alamannenbeute aus dem Rhein bei Neupotz : Plünderungsgut aus dem römischen Gallien*. Mainz: Römisch-Germanischen Zentralmuseum Mainz.

Kuttner, A, Mighall, T, De Vleeschouwer, F, Mauquoy, D, Cortizas, A M, Foster, I D L and Krupp, E A 2014. 'A 3300-year atmospheric metal contamination record from Raeburn Flow raised bog, southwest Scotland', *Journal of Archaeological Science* 44, 1–11.

Laing, L 1994. 'The hoard of Pictish silver from Norrie's Law, Fife', *Studia Celtica* 38, 11–38.

Laing, L 2005. 'The Roman origins of Celtic Christian art', *Archaeological Journal* 162, 146–76.

Laing, L 2010. *European influence on early Celtic art: patrons and artists*. Dublin: Four Courts Press.

Laing, L and Longley, D 2006. *The Mote of Mark. A Dark Age hillfort in south-west Scotland*. Oxford: Oxbow.

Lane, A and Campbell, E 2000. *Dunadd. An early Dalriadic capital*. Oxford: Oxbow.

Lang, J and Holmes, R 1983. 'Studies on the technology of beaded rims on late Roman silver vessels', *Britannia* 14, 197–205.

Lang, J, Hughes, M J and Oddy, W A 1984. 'Report on the scientific examination of the Sea City Dish 62, the Achilles Dish 63 and some other items', in Cahn and Kaufmann-Heinimann (eds) 1984, 375–81.

Lang, J and Hughes, M J 2016. 'The Mildenhall Treasure: technical aspects of construction and decoration', in Hobbs 2016, 240–9.

Lind, L 1981. *Roman denarii found in Sweden 2. Catalogue text*. Stockholm: Almqvist and Wiksell.

McDonnell, G and Milns, J 2015. 'Ferrous and non-ferrous metalworking', in Dockrill et al. 2015, 392–428.

MacGregor, M 1976. *Early Celtic art in north Britain*. Leicester: Leicester University Press.

McKerrell, H 1973. 'Chemical analyses of the silver objects', in Small, Thomas and Wilson 1973, 174–5.

MacKie, E 2000. 'Excavations at Dun Ardtreck, Skye, in 1964 and 1965',

Proceedings of the Society of Antiquaries of Scotland 130, 301–411.

Mackie, E 2016. *Brochs and the Empire: the impact of Rome on Iron Age Scotland as seen in the Leckie broch excavations*. Oxford: Archaeopress.

Magnus, B (ed) 2001. *Roman gold and the development of the early Germanic kingdoms*. Stockholm: Almqvist and Wiksell (Kunglige Vitterhets Historie och Antikvitets Akademien, Konferenser 51).

Mann, J 1974. 'The northern frontier after AD 369', *Glasgow Archaeological Journal* 3, 34–42.

Marshall, F H 1907. *Catalogue of the finger rings, Greek, Etruscan, and Roman, in the Departments of Antiquities, British Museum*. London: British Museum.

Martin, M 2004. 'Childerichs Denare – zum Rückström römischer Silbermünzen ins Merowingerreich', in H Friesinger and A Stuppner (eds), *Zentrum und Peripherie – gesellschaftliche Phänomene in der Frühgeschichte*, 241–78. Wien: Österreichischen Akademie der Wissenschaften (= Mitteilungen der Prähistorischen Kommission 57).

Marzinzik, S 2013. 'The Coleraine treasure from Northern Ireland: a consideration of the fittings', in Hunter and Painter (eds) 2013a, 175–91.

Mattingly, D 2006. *An imperial possession: Britain in the Roman empire, 54 BC–AD 409*. London: Allen Lane.

Maxfield, V 1981. *The military decorations of the Roman army*. London: Batsford.

Mighall, T, Cortizas, A M, Silva Sánchez, N, Foster, I D L, Singh, S, Bateman, M and Pickin, J 2014. 'Identifying evidence for past mining and metallurgy from a record of metal contamination preserved in an ombrotrophic mire near Leadhills, southwest Scotland, UK', *The Holocene* 24, 1719–30.

Moorhead, S n.d. [*c*.2013]. *A history of Roman coinage in Britain*. Witham: Greenlight.

Mráv, Z 2015. 'Maniakion – the golden torc in the late Roman and early Byzantine army: preliminary research report', in T Vida (ed), *The frontier world: Romans, barbarians and military culture. Romania Gothica II*, 287–301. Budapest: Eötvös Loránd University.

Newman, P (ed) 2016. *The archaeology of mining and quarrying in England: a research framework for the archaeology of the extractive industries in England*. National Association of Mining History Organisations. Available at: https://www.namho.org/documents/MINING_FRAMEWORK_Pt_one.pdf [accessed 18/8/2017]

Nieke, M 1993. 'Penannular and related brooches: secular ornament or symbol in action?', in Spearman and Higgitt (eds) 1993, 128–34.

Niemeyer, B 2004. *Die silbernen Halbkugelbecher vom Typ Leuna. Fundkomplexe und Interpretation, Herstellungstechnik und Datierung*. Oxford: Archaeopress (BAR International Series 1250).

Noble, G, Gondek, M, Campbell, E, and Cook, M 2013. 'Between prehistory and history: the archaeological detection of social change among the Picts', *Antiquity* 87 (338), 1136–50.

Noble, G, Goldberg, M and Hamilton, D in preparation. 'The origins of the Pictish symbol system: inscribing identity beyond the edges of Empire'.

Noble, G, Goldberg, M, McPherson, A and Sveinbjarnarson, O 2016. '(Re)discovering the Gaulcross hoard', *Antiquity* 90 (351), 726–41.

Noll, R 1974. 'Eine goldene "Kaiserfibel" aus Niederemmel vom Jahre 316', *Bonner Jahrbücher* 174, 221–44.

Ogden, J 1982. *Jewellery of the ancient world*. London: Trefoil Books.

Ørsnes, M 1988. *Ejsbøl I: Waffenopferfunde des 4.–5. Jahrh. nach Chr.* Copenhagen: Det Kongelige Nordiske Oldskriftselskab.

Painter, K 2010a. 'A silver and glass vessel from the Traprain Law hoard of Hacksilber', *Kölner Jahrbuch* 43, 579–96.

Painter, K 2010b. 'A Roman silver jug with biblical scenes from the treasure found at Traprain Law', in M Henig and N Ramsay (eds), *Intersections: the archaeology and history of Christianity in England, 400–1200. Papers in honour of Martin Biddle and Birthe Kjølbye-Biddle*, 1–23. Oxford: Archaeopress.

Painter, K 2013. 'Hacksilber: a means of exchange?', in Hunter and Painter (eds) 2013a, 215–42.

Pashley, V and Evans, J 2017. 'Lead isotope analysis of lead bar', in R Toolis and C Bowles, *The lost Dark Age kingdom of Rheged. The discovery of a royal stronghold at Trusty's Hill, Galloway*, 49–50. Oxford: Oxbow.

Petrovszky, R (ed) 2006. *Der Barbarenschatz. Geraubt und im Rhein versunken*. Speyer: Historisches Museum der Pfalz/Theiss.

Pickin, J 2010. 'Early lead smelting in southern Scotland', *Historical Metallurgy* 44 (2), 81–4.

Ploumis, I A 2001. 'Gold in political propaganda within the Roman Empire', in Magnus (ed) 2001, 61–80.

Pococke, R 1773. 'An account of some antiquities found in Ireland', *Archaeologia* 2, 32–41.

Pohl, W 1997. *Kingdoms of the Empire: the integration of barbarians in Late Antiquity*. Leiden: Brill (The Transformation of the Roman World 1).

Popović, I 1996. *Les bijoux romains du Musée National de Beograd II. Les bijoux d'or*. Belgrade: National Museum.

Proudfoot, E 1996. 'Excavations at the long cist cemetery on the Hallow Hill, St Andrews, Fife, 1975–7', *Proceedings of the Society of Antiquaries of Scotland* 126, 387–454.

Quast, D 2013. 'Ein kleiner Goldhort der jüngeren römischen Kaiserzeit aus Černivci (ehem. Czernowitz/Cernăuți) in der westlichen Ukraine nebst einigen Anmerkungen zu goldenen Kolbenarmringen', in M Hardt and O Heinrich Tamáska (eds), *Macht des Goldes, Gold der Macht. Herrschafts- und Jenseitsrepräsentation zwischen Antike und Frühmittelalter im mittleren Donauraum*, 171–86. Weinstadt: Verlag Bernhard Albert Greiner.

Quast, D (ed) 2015a. *Das Grab des fränkischen Königs Childerich in Tournai und die Anastasis Childerici vom Jean-Jacques Chifflet aus dem Jahre 1655*. Mainz: RGZM.

Quast, D 2015b. 'Die Grabbeigaben – ein kommentierter Fundkatalog', in Quast (ed) 2015a, 165–85.

Rance, P 2001. 'Attacotti, Déisi and Magnus Maximus: the case for Irish federates in late Roman Britain', *Britannia* 32, 243–70.

Rau, A 2013a. 'Where did the late empire end? Hacksilber and coins in continental and northern Barbaricum c AD 340–500', in Hunter and Painter (eds) 2013a, 339–57.

Rau, A 2013b. 'Some observations on Migration period "Hacksilber" hoards with Roman components', in B Ludowici (ed), *Individual and individuality? Approaches towards an archaeology of personhood in the first millennium AD*, 189–203. Stuttgart: Konrad Theiss Verlag.

Reece, R 1984. 'The use of Roman coinage', *Oxford Journal of Archaeology* 3/2, 197–210.

Reece, R 2002. *The coinage of Roman Britain*. Stroud: Tempus.

Rehren, T and Kraus, K 1999. 'Cupel and crucible: the refining of debased silver in the Colonia Ulpia Traiana, Xanten', *Journal of Roman Archaeology* 12, 263–72.

Ritchie, A 1989. *Picts*. Edinburgh: HMSO.

Ritchie, A 2005. *Kilellan Farm, Ardnave, Islay. Excavation of a prehistoric to early medieval site by Colin Burgess and others*. Edinburgh: Society of Antiquaries of Scotland.

Ritchie, J N G 2002. 'James Curle (1862–1944) and Alexander Ormiston Curle (1866–1955): pillars of the establishment', *Proceedings of the Society of Antiquaries of Scotland* 132, 19–41.

Ritchie, G and Welfare, H 1983. 'Excavations at Ardnave, Islay', *Proceedings of the Society of Antiquaries of Scotland* 113, 302–66.

Roger, J C 1880. 'Notice of a drawing of a bronze crescent-shaped plate, which was dug up at Laws, parish of Monifieth, in 1796', *Proceedings of the Society of Antiquaries of Scotland* 14 (1878–80), 268–74.

Roymans, N 2017. 'Gold, Germanic *foederati* and the end of imperial power in the Late Roman North', in Roymans, Heeren and De Clercq (eds) 2017, 57–80.

Roymans, N and Heeren, S 2015. 'A late Roman *solidus* hoard with *Hacksilber* from Echt (prov. Limburg/NL)', *Archäologisches Korrespondenzblatt* 45/4, 549–62.

Roymans, N, Heeren, S and De Clercq, W (eds) 2017. *Social dynamics in the northwest frontiers of the late Roman empire: beyond decline or transformation*. Amsterdam: Amsterdam University Press

Schot, R, Newman, C and Bhreathnach, E 2011. *Landscapes of cult and kingship*. Dublin: Four Courts Press.

Seipel, W (ed) 1999. *Barbarenschmuck und Römergold. Der Schatz von Szilágysomlyó*. Vienna: Kunsthistorisches Museum.

Semple, S 1998. 'A fear of the past: the place of the prehistoric burial mound in the ideology of middle and later Anglo-Saxon England', in Bradley and Williams (eds) 1998, 109–26.

Semple, S 2013. *Perceptions of the prehistoric in Anglo-Saxon England: religion, ritual and rulership in the landscape*. Oxford: Oxford University Press.

Sheehan, J 2013. 'Hiberno-Scandinavian broad-band arm-rings', in Graham-Campbell 2013, 94–100.

Sheridan, A 2014. 'Gold in ancient Scotland', in Clark 2014, 39–59.

Small, A, Thomas, C and Wilson, D M 1973. *St Ninian's Isle and its treasure*. Oxford: Oxford University Press.

Smith, D J 1960. 'A Roman silver pin from Halton Chesters', *Archaeologia Aeliana* (4th series) 38, 231.

Smith, J 1919. 'Excavation of the forts of Castlehill, Aitnock, and Coalhill, Dalry, Ayrshire', *Proceedings of the Society of Antiquaries of Scotland* 53 (1918–19), 123–34.

Smith, R 2006. 'Radiocarbon dating of early lead smelting sites', *British Mining* 80, 94–110.

Southern, P and Dixon, K R 1999. *The late Roman army*. London: Batsford.

Spearman, M and Higgitt, J (eds) 1993. *The age of migrating ideas: early medieval art in northern Britain and Ireland. Proceedings of the second international conference on Insular art held in the National Museums of Scotland in Edinburgh, 3–6 January 1991*. Edinburgh: National Museums Scotland.

Speidel, M A 1992. 'Roman army pay scales', *Journal of Roman Studies* 82, 87–106.

Stapleton, C P, Freestone, I C and Bowman, S G E 1999. 'Composition and origin of early Mediaeval opaque red enamel from Britain and Ireland', *Journal of Archaeological Science* 26, 913–21.

Stevenson, R B K 1955. 'Pins and the chronology of brochs', *Proceedings of the Prehistoric Society* 21, 282–94.

Stevenson, R B K 1993. 'Further thoughts on some well known problems', in Spearman and Higgitt (eds), 1993.

Stevenson, R B K and Emery, J 1964. 'The Gaulcross hoard of Pictish silver', *Proceedings of the Society of Antiquaries of Scotland* 97 (1963–4), 206–11.

Stos-Gale, Z A and Gale, N H 2009. 'Metal provenancing using isotopes and the Oxford archaeological lead isotope database (OXALID)', *Archaeological and Anthropological Sciences* 1, 195–213.

Stribrny, K 2003. *Funktionanalyse barbarisierter, barbarischer Denare mittels numismatischer und metallurgischer Methoden*. Mainz: von Zabern (=Studien zu Fundmünzen der Antike 18).

Stuart, J 1867. *Sculptured stones of Scotland. Volume second*. Edinburgh: Spalding Club.

Tate, J 1986. 'Some problems in analysing museum material by non-destructive surface sensitive techniques', *Nuclear Instruments and Methods in Physics Research* 14, 20–3.

Tate, J and Troalen, L 2009. *Investigation of the Traprain Law Roman Treasure, EU-Artechexperimental report* (NMS internal report): http://www.eu-artech.org/files/Report_Tate_Troalen.pdf

Taylor, D B 1982. 'Excavation of a promontory fort, broch and souterrain at Hurly Hawkin, Angus', *Proceedings of the Society of Antiquaries of Scotland* 112, 215–53.

Thomas, C 1995. 'The artist and the people, a foray into uncertain semiotics', in C Bourke (ed), *From the isles of the north: Early Medieval art in northern Britain* 1–7. Belfast: HMSO.

Tissot, I, Monteiro, O C, Barreiros, M A, Corregidor, V, Correia, J and Guerra, M F 2016. 'Corrosion of silver alloys in sulphide environments: a multianalytical approach for surface characterization', *RSC Advances* 6, 51856–63.

Tylecote, R F 1986. *The prehistory of metallurgy in the British Isles*. London: Institute of Metals.

Vogt, M 2006. *Spangenhelme: Baldenheim und verwandte Typen*. Mainz: Römisch-Germanischen Zentralmuseums

Voß, H-U 2013. 'Roman silver in "Free Germany": Hacksilber in context', in Hunter and Painter (eds) 2013a, 305–19.

Vulić, H, Doračić, D, Hobbs, R and Lang, J 2017. 'The Vinkovci treasure of Late Roman silver plate: a preliminary report', Journal of Roman Archaeology 30 (forthcoming).

Ward-Perkins, B 2005. *The fall of Rome and the end of civilisation*. Oxford: Oxford University Press.

Watson, W J 1926. *The history of the Celtic placenames of Scotland*. Edinburgh: Blackwood.

Way, A 1849. 'Notices of a remarkable discovery of silver ornaments in a tumulus at Largo, in Fifeshire', *Archaeological Journal* 6, 248–59.

Webster, L and Backhouse, J (eds) 1991. *The making of England: Anglo-Saxon art and culture AD 600–900*. London: British Museum.

Wedlake, W J 1982. *The Excavation of the Shrine of Apollo at Nettleton, Wiltshire, 1965–1971*. London: Society of Antiquaries of London.

White, S, Manley, J, Jones, R, Orna-Ornstein, J, Johns, C and Webster, L 1999. 'A mid-fifth century hoard of Roman and pseudo-Roman material from Patching, West Sussex', *Britannia* 30, 301–14.

Whitfield, N 1993. 'The filigree of the Hunterston and "Tara" brooches', in Spearman and Higgitt (eds) 1993, 118–27.

Whitfield, N 1997. 'Filigree animal ornament from Ireland and Scotland of the late seventh to ninth centuries', in C E Karkov, R T

Farrell and M Ryan (eds), *The Insular tradition*, 211–43. New York: University of New York Press.

Whitfield, N 2001. 'The "Tara" brooch: an emblem of Irish status in its European context', in C Hourihane (ed), *From Ireland coming*, 211–48. Princeton: Index of Christian Art.

Whitfield, N 2004. 'More thoughts on the wearing of brooches in early medieval Ireland', in C Hourihane (ed), *Irish art historical studies in honour of Peter Harbison*, 70–108. Dublin: Four Courts.

Whitfield, N 2007. 'Motifs and techniques in early medieval Celtic filigree: their ultimate origins', in R Moss (ed), *Making and meaning in Insular art: proceedings of the fifth international conference on Insular art held at Trinity College, Dublin, 25–28 August 2005*, 18–39. Dublin: Trinity College.

Whitfield, N 2013. 'Hunterston/"Tara" type brooches reconsidered', in Hawkes (ed) 2013, 145–61.

Wieczorek, W and Périn, P (eds) 2001. *Das Gold der Barbarenfürsten. Schätze aus Prunkgräbern des 5. Jahrhunderts n. Chr. zwischen Kaukasus und Gallien*. Stuttgart: Theiss.

Williams, H 1998. 'Monuments and the past in early Anglo-Saxon England', in Bradley and Williams (eds) 1998, 90–108.

Wilson, A 2001. 'The Novantae and Romanization in Galloway', *Transactions of the Dumfriesshire and Galloway Natural History and Antiquarian Society* 75, 73–131.

Wilson, G V and Flett, J S 1921. *The lead, zinc, copper and nickel ores of Scotland*. London: HMSO (Special Report on the Mineral resources of Great Britain 17).

Woolliscroft, D J 2017. 'The Elginhaugh coin hoard and the date of the first Roman invasion of Scotland', in A Parker (ed), *Ad Vallum: papers on the Roman army and frontiers in celebration of Dr Brian Dobson*, 75–81. Oxford: BAR (BAR British Series 631).

Yeroulanou, A 1999. *Diatrita. Pierced-work gold jewellery from the 3rd to the 7th century*. Athens: Benaki Museum.

Youngs, S (ed) 1989. *'The work of angels': masterpieces of Celtic metalwork, 6th–9th centuries AD*. London: British Museum.

Youngs, S 2005. 'After Oldcroft: a British silver pin from Welton le Wold, Lincolnshire', in N Crummy (ed), *Image, craft and the Classical world: essays in honour of Donald Bailey and Catherine Johns*, 249–54. Montagnac: Editions Monique Mergoil.

Youngs, S 2009. 'From metalwork to manuscript: some observations on the use of Celtic art in Insular manuscripts', *Anglo-Saxon Studies in History and Archaeology* 16, 45–64.

Youngs, S 2010. 'A copper alloy dress pin', in P Bennett, I Riddler and C Sparey-Green, *The Roman watermills and settlement at Ickham, Kent*, 181–5. Canterbury: Canterbury Archaeological Trust (The Archaeology of Canterbury, new series 5).

Youngs, S 2013. 'From chains to brooches: the uses and hoarding of silver in north Britain in the Early Historic period', in Hunter and Painter (eds) 2013a, 403–25.

Youngs, S 2016. 'Silver handpins from the West Country to Scotland: perplexing portable antiquities', in F Hunter and A Sheridan (eds), *Ancient Lives: object, people and place in early Scotland. Essays for David V Clarke on his 70th birthday*, 303–16. Leiden: Sidestone Press.

Scotland's Early Silver
Exhibited objects

Listed below are the objects exhibited in *Scotland's Early Silver* at the National Museum of Scotland, 13 October 2017–25 February 2018. They are listed under case titles and in display order. All are silver unless stated otherwise.

SILVER, NOT GOLD

- Roman wash basin fragment, Traprain Law Treasure, East Lothian, National Museums Scotland accession no. X.GVA 44
- Roman plate fragment, Traprain Law Treasure, X.GVA 161
- Roman hacksilver parcel, Traprain Law Treasure, X.GVA 142 D
- Roman gold *solidi* and silver *siliquae*, findspots unknown, H.C263–5, 267–8, 11042–9, 11051–2, 11054, 11066, 14496, A.1922.531–3
- Early Medieval brooch, Tummel Bridge, Perth and Kinross, X.FC 162
- Early Medieval brooch, continental Europe, precise findspot unknown, X.FD 35

SCOTLAND'S EARLIEST SILVER

- Roman penannular brooch, Newstead, Scottish Borders, X.FRA 812
- Roman necklace, Newstead, X.FRA 851
- Roman silver and bronze coins, Newstead, H.C11719, 11721, 11723, 14609, 14611, 14628, 14646, 14657, 14662, 14668, 14672, 14678, 14683, 14685, 14704, 14706, 14714, 14715, 14721, 14723, 14726, 14731, 14736, 14747, 14753, 14756, 14758, 14777, 14809, 14817, 19131
- Roman miniature votive strainer, Traprain Law, X.GVM 261
- Roman trumpet brooch, Cappuck, Scottish Borders, X.FT 122
- Roman trumpet brooch, Ayrshire, X.FG 9
- Roman finger-rings, Culbin Sands, Moray, X.BI 25639, X.BI 29463
- Roman silver-coated copper-alloy harness mount, Newstead, X.FRA 525

BRIBERY ON THE FRONTIER

- Two hoards of Roman *denarii* and the Iron Age pots which contained them, Birnie, Moray, X.2006.22
- Ceramic mould for making fake Roman coins, Brighouse Bay, Dumfries and Galloway, X.1997.770

CHANGING TIMES

- Hoard of Roman hacksilver, Dairsie, Fife, X.FRH 1–4

HACKING SILVER

- Selection of Roman hacksilver from the Traprain Law Treasure, East Lothian, X.GVA 3, 4, 13, 16, 19C, 24, 28A, 31A, 36, 38A, 51, 59A, 59C, 63A–B, 68B, 74A, 75, 80B, 82, 85, 87A, 100, 101A, 104–5, 108, 123A–B, 142A–C, 143, 147, 149, 152A–D, 160–1, 163
- Late Iron Age ceramic crucible, Traprain Law, X.GVM 574
- Late Iron Age mount, Traprain Law, X.GVM 269
- Late Iron Age handpin head, Traprain Law, X.GVM 120
- Late Iron Age pin shaft, Traprain Law, X.GVM 202
- Late Iron Age spiral finger-ring, Traprain Law, X.GVM 153
- Late Iron Age tinned copper-alloy brooch, Traprain Law, X.GVM 91
- Late Iron Age projecting-headed pin, Sculptor's Cave, Covesea, Moray, X.HM 69
- Late Iron Age tweezers, Sculptor's Cave, Covesea, X.HM 79

MANAGING SILVER

- Early Medieval handpin, bangle and loop-in-loop chain, Gaulcross, Aberdeenshire, IL.2001.1.2–4 (on loan from Aberdeenshire Council Museums)
- Ninety fragments of Roman and Early Medieval hacksilver, recovered in 2013, Gaulcross (not yet allocated to a museum)

BURYING SILVER

– Early Medieval hacksilver hoard, Norrie's Law, Fife, X.FC 26–126, 309–22

CONSPICUOUS CONSUMPTION

– Late Iron Age / Early Medieval massive chain, Hoardweel, Scottish Borders, IL.2009.15.5 (on loan from Douglas and Angus Estates)
– Late Iron Age / Early Medieval massive chain, Torvean, Inverness, Highland, X.FC 148
– Late Iron Age / Early Medieval massive chain, Haddington, East Lothian, X.FC 149
– Late Iron Age / Early Medieval massive chain, Traprain Law, East Lothian, X.FC 248
– Late Iron Age / Early Medieval massive chain, Borland, South Lanarkshire, X.FC 264
– Late Iron Age / Early Medieval massive chain, Whitecleugh, South Lanarkshire, X.FC 150
– Late Iron Age / Early Medieval massive chain, Parkhill, Aberdeenshire, X.FC 147
– Late Iron Age / Early Medieval massive chain, Whitlaw, Scottish Borders, X.FC 172
– Late Iron Age / Early Medieval massive chain, Nigg Bay, Aberdeenshire, ABDUA 15644 (on loan from University of Aberdeen Museums)

HOLDING IT ALL TOGETHER

– Early Medieval brooch fragment, Gaulcross, Aberdeenshire (not yet allocated to a museum)
– Early Medieval brooch, Norrie's Law, Fife, X.FC 36
– Early Medieval brooch, Tummel Bridge, Perth and Kinross, X.FC 164
– Early Medieval tinned copper-alloy brooch, Castlehill, North Ayrshire, X.HH 339
– Early Medieval brooch, St Ninian's Isle hoard, Shetland, X.FC 286
– Early Medieval brooch, St Ninian's Isle hoard, X.FC 295
– Early Medieval brooch, Aldclune, Perth and Kinross, X.FC 304
– Early Medieval brooch, Croy, Inverness, Highland, X.FC 13
– Early Medieval brooch, Rogart, Sutherland, Highland, X.FC 1
– Early Medieval brooches, Clunie, Perth and Kinross, X.FC 176–7, 305

SILVER AND GOLD

– Early Medieval brooch, Hunterston, North Ayrshire, X.FC 8

FRESH SUPPLIES

– Early Medieval bowl, St Ninian's Isle, Shetland, X.FC 270
– Viking Age brooch, Skaill, Orkney, X.IL 742
– Viking Age hacked ring-money fragments, Burray, Orkney, X.IL 271
– Viking Age ring-money, Burray, X.IL 242–4
– Viking Age ingots, Cuerdale, Lancashire, X.IM 24–6
– Islamic *dirhams* from a Viking hacksilver hoard, Storr Rock, Skye, H.C9683
– Anglo-Saxon and Viking coins, Storr Rock, Skye, H.C18475, 18508–9, 18517, 18524, 18544–5, 18559, 18571, 18584

EXHIBITED OBJECTS

Index

Alva, silver deposits 5
Anglo-Saxon 112–14, 116, 120, 133, 140, 145–7
– brooch, Chessell Down, Isle of Wight 115
– buckle, Sutton Hoo 114; 115
arm-rings
– Cove, Dumfries and Galloway, Roman 56–7; 57
– Galloway hoard, Viking 133; 133
– Gaulcross hoard, Aberdeenshire, Early Medieval 77, 80, 83, 104; 77, 82
– Hallow Hill, Fife, Roman 13
– Macduff, Aberdeenshire, Roman 13; 14
– Norrie's Law hoard, Fife, Early Medieval 87, 90, 92, 104, 145; 88
– Viking 131–3, 140, 146; 132, 140
Athelstaneford, East Lothian, brooch 13
Ayrshire, Roman brooch 12, 17, 108; 108

balance beam, Croy hoard, Inverness-shire 122; 122
bangles (see arm-rings)
basins (see vessels)
Bathgate Hills, silver deposits 5
belt buckle, fittings
– Coleraine, Northern Ireland 73; 72
– Gaulcross hoard 78; 80
– Sutton Hoo 114, 115
– Traprain Law Treasure 51, 114; 51
– Vermand, Aisne, France 73; 73
Birnie, Moray 19, 21, 27–9; 20, 22, 27–9, 31
Birrens, Dumfries and Galloway, gold medallion 56; 56
Blair Drummond, Stirling, torcs 103; 103

Borland, South Lanarkshire, massive silver chain 97; 94, 96–7, 99
bowls (see vessels)
bracelets (see arm-rings)
Brighouse Bay, Dumfries and Galloway, counterfeit coin mould 23
brooches
– Crichton, Midlothian 109
– Early Medieval 72, 80, 95, 104, 107–24, 127, 131, 140, 145
– Brough of Birsay, Orkney, mould 119; 120
– Castlehill, Ayrshire 74, 109; 110
– Chessell Down, Isle of Wight 115
– Clatchard Craig, Fife, mould 113
– Clunie hoard, Perth and Kinross 113; XIV, 106, 113, 115
– Croy hoard, Inverness, Highland 114, 122; 116, 122
– Dunadd, Argyll 107–8, 113, 119, 107, 111–2
– Freswick Links, Caithness 119; 119
– Galloway hoard 133
– Gaulcross hoard, Aberdeenshire 77, 80, 109; 81, 110
– Hunterston, North Ayrshire 116–8, 120–2, 116–8, 121
– Norrie's Law hoard, Fife 87, 90–1, 109; 87
– St Ninian's Isle hoard, Shetland 119, 127–8; 115, 119–20, 128
– Tummel Bridge, Perth and Kinross 109–11; 110, XVI
– unknown continental findspot XVI

– Westness, Orkney 140
– Iron Age 108
– Roman 12, 28, 102, 108–9; 31
– Athelstaneford, East Lothian, trumpet 13
– Ayrshire, trumpet 108; 12, 17, 108
– Birnie, Moray 31
– Cappuck, Scottish Borders, trumpet 17
– Carn Liath, Sutherland, crossbow 13, 35; 35
– crossbow 13, 35, 56–7, 108, 146
– Erickstanebrae, Dumfries and Galloway, crossbow 56; 56
– Moray Firth, crossbow 57; 58
– Newstead, Scottish Borders, penannular 17
– penannular 13, 74, 108–9
– Tarland, Aberdeenshire, penannular 13
– Traprain Law, East Lothian, penannular 73–4; 74
– trumpet 12–13, 17, 108; 17, 108
– Viking 130–2, 140, 146
– Galloway hoard 133; 131
– Skaill hoard, Orkney 130–1; 131, 134
Brook and Son, George Street, Edinburgh 46, 63–4; 63–4
Brough of Birsay, Orkney, mould 119; 120
buckle (see belt buckle, fittings)
Buist, George 84–6
bullion (see silver, bullion)
Burray, Orkney, hacksilver hoard 132
Byzantine Empire 133

Caerleon, Gwent, copper-alloy chain 102
Capledrae, Fife, Roman ring 13, 35, 38; *35*
Cappuck, Scottish Borders, Roman brooch *17*
Carn Liath, Sutherland, Roman brooch 13, 35; *35*
Castlehill, North Ayrshire, Early Medieval brooch 74, 109; *110*
chains
- copper-alloy 102–3; *103*
- massive silver XV, 74, 83, 91, 95–104, 108, 111, 132, 139, 143; *XIV, 96–7, 139, 142*
  - dating of 101–4
  - Pictish symbols 100–101
  - surviving examples
    - Borland, South Lanarkshire 97; *94, 96–7, 99*
    - Haddington, East Lothian 97; *96–7, 98*
    - Hoardweel, Scottish Borders 99, 102; *96–7, 99, 143*
    - Parkhill, Aberdeenshire 97, 101; *96–7, 98, 99, 100, 143*
    - Nigg Bay, Aberdeenshire 95; *96–7*
    - Torvean, Inverness-shire 97, 99, 104; *96–7, 98*
    - Traprain Law, East Lothian 74, 104; *96–7, 104*
    - Whitecleugh, South Lanarkshire 101; *96–7, 99, 100, 101*
    - Whitlaw, Scottish Borders *96–7, 99*
- Roman silver, Gaulcross, Aberdeenshire 77, 80; *77, 83*
- Roman silver, Great Chesters, Northumberland 102
Chaourse, Picardy, France, Roman silver vessel hoard 39; *39*

Childeric, *denarii* in grave 26
chip-carved metalwork 73, 114
Clatchard Craig hillfort, Fife 83, 113
Clunie hoard, Perth and Kinross 113; *XIV, 106, 113, 115*
coins (*see* also hoards / hoarding)
- Anglo-Saxon 122, 129, 146; *122, 129*
- David I, King 3–5; *5*
- dirhams 129, 146; *129*
- Roman
  - *denarii* XIII, 12, 15, 19–26, 34, 58, 140, 145; *10, 12, 15, 17, 18, 25, 138, 142*
  - double-*denarii* / radiate 34
  - *siliquae* 59–60, 80; *60, 80*
  - *solidi* 53–4, 56; *XV, 55, 56*
  - counterfeit moulds 22; *23*
Coleraine, Northern Ireland, Roman hacksilver hoard 73; *72*
Commodus, campaigns in Scotland 20
Count of the Sacred Largesse 54
Cove, Dumfries and Galloway, gold armlet 56; *57*
Covesea, Sculptor's Cave, Moray, tweezers and pin 69; *70*
crossbow brooches (*see* brooches, Roman)
Croy, Inverness-shire, hoard 114, 122; *116, 122*
crucibles (*see* silver-working)
Cuerdale, Lancashire, Viking hacksilver hoard 130; *134*
Culbin Sands, Moray, Roman silver ring 13, 36; *14, 17, 35*
cups (*see* vessels)
Curle, Alexander O 45–6

Dairsie, Fife, Roman hacksilver hoard 33, 36–40, 83, 102, 142; *XII, XIV, 32–3, 36–8*
David I, coin 3–5; *5*
denarii (*see* coins, Roman)

Denmark, hacksilver hoards 73, 92, 146; *91, 147*
diplomacy (*see* Roman, policy / payments)
Dunadd, Argyll 107–8, 113, 119, 145; *107, 111–2*

Early Medieval (*see* also brooches; hacksilver; hoards / hoarding; Anglo-Saxon)
- kingdoms XIII, 90, 92, 118–19, 140
ear-rings, Traprain Law 13
East Wemyss, Fife, Pictish symbols 101
Echt, Netherlands, Roman coin and hacksilver hoard 52; *52*
Ejsbøl, Denmark, offering site 73
Elginhaugh, Midlothian, Roman fort and coin hoard 15; *15*
enamel, use of 71–2, 85
Erickstanebrae, Dumfries and Galloway, Roman brooch 56; *56*

Falkirk, Stirlingshire, Roman *denarius* hoard *XIV, 18, 25, 138*
Fife, Roman policy towards 40
finger-rings 108–9
- gold
  - Philiphaugh, Scottish Borders 57; *58*
- silver
  - Capledrae, Fife, Roman 13, 35, 38; *35*
  - Culbin Sands, Moray, Roman 13, 36; *14, 17, 35*
  - Luce Sands, Dumfries and Galloway, Roman 13
  - Newgrange, Co. Meath 92; *92*
  - Norrie's Law hoard, Fife 87, 92, 145; *74, 87*
  - Traprain Law, East Lothian, Roman 13
flagons (*see* vessels)

Freswick Links, Caithness, Early Medieval brooch 119; *119*

galena (*see* also mines/mining) 3, 4
Galloway hoard 133; *131, 133, 134*
garnet 114, 116–7, 146
Gaulcross, Aberdeenshire, hacksilver hoard 38, 77–83, 84, 87, 90–2, 104, 109, 130, 139, 141, 143–6; *4, 77, 79–83*
gilding 49, 61–2, 113–4
goblets 50
gold 53–8, 104, 107, 113, 140, 145
– Early Medieval filigree decoration 114, 116–7, 122; *115–7, 140*
– Roman
　– armlet, Cove, Dumfries and Galloway 56; *57*
　– brooch, Erickstanebrae, Dumfries and Galloway 56; *56*
　– brooch, Moray Firth 57; *58*
　– coins 11, 52, 54–8; *52*
　– medallion, Birrens, Dumfries and Galloway 56; *56*
　– ring, Philiphaugh, Scottish Borders 57; *58*
– Viking Age Galloway hoard 133
Great Chesters, Northumberland, Roman silver chain 102
Großbodungen, Germany, hacksilver and coin hoard 54

hacksilver XIV, 6, 111
– distribution 54, 56, 141, 145–6; *142*
– hoards
　– Burray, Orkney, Viking *132*
　– Coleraine, Northern Ireland, Roman 73; *72*
　– Dairsie, Fife, Roman 33, 36–40, 83, 102; *32–3, 36–8*

– Echt, Netherlands, Roman 52; *52*
– Galloway hoard, Early Medieval and Viking Age 133; *131, 133, 134*
– Gaulcross, Aberdeenshire, Roman and Early Medieval 38, 77–83, 84, 87, 90–2, 104, 109, 130, 139, 141, 143–6; *4, 77, 79–83*
– Großbodungen, Germany, Roman 54
– Mannerup, Denmark, Roman and Early Medieval 91; *91, 147*
– Norrie's Law, Fife, Roman and Early Medieval 7, 38, 84–92, 102, 104, 109, 130, 139, 141, 143–6; *2, 71, 76, 84, 85–9, 144*
– Skaill, Orkney, Viking 130; *131, 134*
– Storr Rock, Skye, Viking *129*
– Traprain Law Treasure, East Lothian, Roman 6, 7, 34, 45–51, 53, 58–60, 80, 83, 87, 102, 114, 140; *XV, 4, 8, 44–51, 136, 138*
– motives 39–40, 51–4
– standard weights 51–3
Haddington, East Lothian, massive silver chain 97; *96–7, 98*
Hallow Hill, Fife, Roman bracelet 13
Halton Chesters, Northumberland, silver pin 72; *72*
handpins (*see* pins)
helmet
– Morken, Nordrhein-Westfalen, Germany *89*
– Norrie's Law, Fife, possible fragment 89, 102, 139, 144
High Pasture Cave, Skye, copper-alloy chain *103*
Hilton of Cadboll, cross-slab 113; *118*
hoards/hoarding
– *denarius* (*see* also coins, Roman; Birnie; Elginhaugh; Falkirk)

– in Scotland 15, 19–26, 111, 138, 145; *15, 18, 25, 18, 25, 138, 142*
– elsewhere 21, 145
– Early Medieval
　– Clunie hoard, Perth and Kinross 113; *106, 113, 115*
　– Croy, Inverness-shire 114, 122; *116, 122*
　– Galloway hoard 133; *131, 133, 134*
　– Gaulcross, Aberdeenshire, hacksilver hoard 38, 77–83, 84, 87, 90–92, 104, 109, 130, 139, 141, 143–6; *4, 77, 79–83*
　– Norrie's Law, Fife, hacksilver 7, 38, 84–92, 102, 104, 109, 130, 139, 141, 143–6; *2, 71, 76, 84, 85–9, 144*
　– St Ninian's Isle, Shetland 119, 127–8; *115, 119–20, 126, 128*
– hacksilver (*see* hacksilver, hoards)
– interpretation of (*see* also Prehistoric monuments, reuse of) 147–6
– Viking Age
　– Burray, Orkney *132*
　– Iona, Argyll 128
　– Croy, Inverness-shire 114, 122; *116, 122*
　– Galloway hoard 133; *131, 133, 134*
　– Skaill, Orkney 130; *131, 134*
　– Storr Rock, Skye *129*
Hoardweel, Scottish Borders, massive silver chain 99, 102; *96–7, 99*
Hunterston brooch 116–8, 120–2; *116–8, 121*

imported pottery and glass, post-Roman 111–2, 145; *111*
ingots
– gold 133
– lead 5
– silver 61, 80, 83, 90, 113, 128, 133; *82*

inscriptions
– on stone 112
– runic 121; *121*
Insular art 112–9, 146
Iona, Argyll, Viking Age hoard 128
Iron Age (*see also* brooches, Iron Age; torcs)
– impact of silver on 25–6
– settlements 19, 21, 26–7, 102
Islamic world, coinage (*see* coins, *dirhams*)

Jedburgh, Scottish Borders, gold coin 55

Leckie, Stirlingshire, chain 102
lead 3, 5–6
Leadhills 5
Lindisfarne Gospels 113
Luce Sands, Dumfries and Galloway, Roman finger-ring 13

Macduff, Aberdeenshire, Roman bracelet 13; *14*
Mannerup, Denmark, hacksilver hoard 91; *91*
Manor Valley, Scottish Borders, lead processing 6
massive silver chains (*see* chains, massive silver)
medallion, gold 56–7; *56*
metalworking (*see* silver-working)
metal-detecting 19, 21, 27–8, 33–4, 36, 38, 50, 78
mines / mining 3, 5–6
Moray Firth, brooch from 57; *58*
Mote of Mark, Galloway, hillfort 6, 119
moulds (*see* silver-working)
mounts
– Gaulcross hoard, Aberdeenshire 80, 144; *81*
– Nettleton, Wiltshire 80

– Norrie's Law hoard, Fife 87, 144; *88*
– Traprain Law, East Lothian 69

necklace, Newstead, Scottish Borders *13*
Nettleton, Wiltshire, mounts 80
Neupotz, Germany, Roman river find 54
Newgrange, Co. Meath, offerings and finger-rings 56, 92; *92*
Newstead, Scottish Borders, Roman fort *10, 12, 13, 17, 23*
niello 38, 49, 61
Nigg Bay, Aberdeenshire, massive silver chain 95; *96–7*
Norrie's Law, Fife, hacksilver hoard 7, 38, 84–92, 102, 104, 109, 130, 139, 141, 143–6; *2, 71, 76, 84, 85–9, 144*

Oldcroft, Gloucestershire, pin and coin hoard 70; *71*

Parkhill, Aberdeenshire, massive silver chain 97, 101; *96–7, 98, 99, 100*
Patching, Sussex, Roman coin and hacksilver hoard 52
Philiphaugh, Scottish Borders, Roman finger-ring 57
Pictish symbols
– in caves 101
– on silver 35, 84, 85–6, 89, 101–2, 143–4; *85–6, 89, 100, 101, 143*
– on stone 35, 84, 100–2; *100*
Picts, emergence of 26, 40, 91, 101
pins 28, 69, 108–9; *31, 70, 133*
– disc-headed 102; *102*
– proto-handpins and handpins 69–73, 77, 84–6, 90; *71, 72, 77, 82, 85, 86*
– zoomorphic 72; *72*
Prehistoric monuments, reuse 35, 38, 77–8, 91–2, 130, 146–7

replicas
– Norrie's Law 85–6
– Traprain Law 63–4
Rhynie, Aberdeenshire 112
rings (*see* finger-rings)
ring-money 132; *132*
Roman (*see also* gold, Roman)
– coins (*see* coins, Roman)
– hacksilver (*see* hacksilver)
– military pay 11–12, 53–4
– policy / payments XIII, XV, 20–6, 57, 138, 145–6
– silver from Iron Age sites 13, 35, 36, 38; *14, 17, 35*

St Ninian's Isle, Shetland, hoard 119, 127; *115, 119–20, 126, 128*
scientific analysis 5, 7, 61–2, 69, 85–6, 102, 112–13, 127; *61–2*
Septimius Severus
– campaigns in Scotland 23–5
– propaganda coins 24
siliquae (*see* coins, Roman)
silver (*see also* hacksilver; mines / mining; Roman, policy / payments; silver-working; tinning)
– bullion 6, 39, 40, 50, 53–4, 83–4, 102, 122, 128, 130, 133
silver-working
– crucibles 3, 22, 69, 108, 113, 145; *4, 70, 144*
– moulds 22, 113, 119; *107, 112, 120, 144*
– recycling XIII, XV–XVI, 6–7, 22, 72, 74, 80, 83, 90–1, 94 –5, 104, 127, 138–9
Skaill, Orkney, Viking hacksilver hoard 130; *131, 134*
slavery 130
smelting (*see* lead)
solidi (*see* coins, Roman)

INDEX

167

Pages 169, 170, 172–3: Details from the hacksilver hoards found at Norrie's Law, Fife, Dairsie, Fife, and Traprain Law, East Lothian.

spoon, Roman
– Gaulcross 80; *80*
– Traprain Law Treasure 49–50; *49*
Storr Rock, Skye, Viking hoard *129*
strainer, Traprain Law, East Lothian 13
strap ends (*see* belt buckle, fittings)
Sutton Hoo, Suffolk 114, 116; *115*
sword-fittings 73; *72*

tableware (*see* vessels)
'Tara' brooch, Ireland 117
Tarland, Aberdeenshire, Roman brooch 13
tinning, in imitation of silver 139
– Castlehill, Ayrshire, brooch 109; *110*
– Traprain Law, pins/brooch 73–4; *74*
torcs 103–4, 108–9; *103, 109*
– Blair Drummond, Stirling 103
Torvean, Inverness-shire, massive silver chain 97, 99, 104; *96–7, 98*

Traprain Law, East Lothian
– finds 13, 41–2, 54, 69, 73–4; *14, 17, 41–2, 70, 74*
– massive silver chain 74, 104; *96–7, 104*
– Traprain Treasure
– replica 63–4
– Roman hacksilver 6, 7, 34, 45–51, 53, 58–60, 80, 83, 87, 102, 114, 140; *XV, 4, 8, 44–51, 136, 138*
– scientific analysis 61–2
Trimontium (*see* Newstead)
Trusty's Hill, Galloway 6
Tummel Bridge, Perthshire, hoard including brooches 109–111; *110*
tweezers, Covesea, Sculptor's Cave, Moray 69; *70*

unknown continental findspot, Early Medieval brooch *XVI*

Vermand, Aisne, France, buckle 73; *73*
vessels 80, 87, 90, 92; *80, 88*
– Early Medieval (*see* Norrie's Law; St Ninian's Isle)
– Roman silver 12 (*see* Chaourse; Dairsie; Echt; Gaulcross; Großbodungen; Traprain Treasure; Water Newton)
Viking Age 128–33

Wanlockhead 5, *4*
Water Newton, Cambridgeshire, hoard 52
Westness, Orkney, Early Medieval brooch *140*
Whitecleugh, South Lanarkshire, massive silver chain 101; *96–7, 99, 100, 101*
Whithorn, Dumfries and Galloway 111
Whitlaw, Scottish Borders, massive silver chain *96–7, 99*

Acknowledgements

The publisher is grateful to the following sources for permission to use their objects, images or text within this publication. No reproduction of material in copyright is permitted without prior contact with the publisher or with the original sources.

IMAGE CREDITS

© NATIONAL MUSEUMS SCOTLAND
for all images used within this book, except for the following:

COURTESY OF ABERDEENSHIRE COUNCIL MUSEUMS
Image © National Museums Scotland – for Figure 7.1

UNIVERSITY OF ABERDEEN MUSEUMS
Image © National Museums Scotland – for Figure 2.5

BAYERISCHES STAATSBIBLIOTHEK MÜNCHEN – for Figure 5.16

THE BRITISH MUSEUM
© Trustees of the British Museum
for Figures 4.11, 4.12, 4.13, 5.22, 6.4a, 6.7, 8.12, 9.15, 9.16, 10.10

FIFE CULTURAL TRUST COLLECTION
Image © National Museums Scotland
for Figures 4.3, 7.21, 7.22, 7.23

BY COURTESY OF THE FAMILY OF A O CURLE
Image © National Museums Scotland – for Figure 5.35 a, b

GDKE, LANDESMUSEUM MAINZ (U. RUDISCHER)
for Figure 9.4

JÜRGEN VOGEL, LVR LANDESMUSEUM, BONN
for Figure 7.32

LANDESAMT FÜR DENKMALPFLEGE UND ARCHÄOLOGIE SACHSEN-ANHALT, JURAJ LIPTÁK – for Figure 5.17

LOS ANGELES COUNTY MUSEUM
Image © Museum Associates/LACMA – for Figure 5.20

MORAY AERIAL SURVEY
Barri Jones / Ian Keillar – for Figure 3.9

THE METROPOLITAN MUSEUM OF ART, NEW YORK (THOMAS J WATSON LIBRARY)
© Photo SCALA, Florence 2017
for Figure 6.8

NATIONAL MUSEUM OF IRELAND
© Reproduced with the kind permission of the National Museum of Ireland – for Figure 7.33

© MUSEUM ORGANISATION ROMU
for Figure 7.34, 11.11

SOCIETY OF ANTIQUARIES OF NEWCASTLE UPON TYNE / GREAT NORTH MUSEUM – for Figure 6.6

RELICARTE
Prepared by Relicarte for National Museums Scotland
for Figure 5.6b

COURTESY VRIJE UNIVERSITEIT, AMSTERDAM – for Figure 5.15

With grateful thanks to the curators, conservators, photographers, picture library and publishing staff, collections services, exhibition, design and administrative staff who have contributed to this book.